PREACHING
THE PSALMS

Preaching
the Psalms

J. Clinton McCann, Jr.
& James C. Howell

Abingdon Press

Nashville

PREACHING THE PSALMS

Library of Congress Cataloging-in-Publication Data

McCann, J. Clinton, 1951-
Preaching the Psalms / J. Clinton McCann, Jr. & James C. Howell.
p. cm.
ISBN 0-687-04499-5 (alk. paper)
1. Bible. O.T. Psalms—Homiletical use. I. Howell, James C., 1955- II. Title.

BS1430.55 .M33 2001
251—dc21

2001027920

01 02 03 04 05 06 07 08 09 10—10 9 8 7 6 5 4 3 2 1

With deep gratitude,
we dedicate this volume to our
teacher, mentor, and friend,
Roland E. Murphy, O. Carm.,
a wise and compassionate
exemplar of what it means
to delight in the Lord's instruction
(Psalm 1:2)

Contents

Acknowledgments

Any book is a communal endeavor, but this is especially the case with a co-authored volume. I am grateful to James Howell for the friendship, cooperation, and mutual commitment to the Psalms as Scripture that led to and are embodied in this book. Our combined efforts demonstrate what is possible when church and academy work together. James and I began studying the Psalms together at Duke University, including one semester during which we spent an evening each week reading through the entire Psalter in Hebrew under the leadership of Professor Orval Wintermute, whose love for the language and the Psalms has remained an inspiration to me.

What has turned out to be a life-long involvement with the Book of Psalms was also inspired and strongly encouraged by our professor, mentor, and dissertation advisor, Father Roland E. Murphy, O. Carm., to whom this book is gratefully dedicated. From Father Murphy, we learned not only how to think critically about the Psalms but also to treasure them as a repository of wisdom and instruction about God and humankind, as well as a source of comfort and challenge to Jews and Christians throughout thousands of years.

Chapters 6–8 of this volume were delivered in a slightly different form as the 1998 Todd Lectures at Memphis Theological Seminary. I am grateful to Memphis Seminary for the invitation to be the Todd Lecturer, as well as for the kind hospitality and gracious responses that I received. The lectures served as an impetus for me to bring together in a new and formal way the material that had served as a basis for teaching and learning about the Psalms at Eden Theological Seminary and in a variety of congregational and ecclesiastical settings.

So, I want to thank also my students and colleagues at Eden Seminary, as well as persons in the following congregations or church organizations with whom I have taught and learned about the Psalms during the time that this book has been in process: Kirkwood (Mo.) United Church of Christ (UCC); Illinois Valley

Mission Council, Illinois Conference, UCC; Southeast Association, Wisconsin Conference, UCC; First Presbyterian Church, Gastonia, N.C.; St. John's UCC (Mehlville, Mo.); Trinity Presbyterian Church (Little Rock, Ark.); Eliot Chapel (Kirkwood, Mo.); Immanual UCC (Ferguson, Mo.); Webster Groves (Mo.) Presbyterian Church; First Congregational UCC (Webster Groves (Mo.); Conclvae XV (a gathering of pastors in Grand Rapids, Mich.); First United Methodist Church (O'Fallon, Ill.); Michigan Conference, UCC; St. Mark Presbyterian Church (Ballwin, Mo.); Eastern Association, Ohio Conference, UCC; St. Paul UCC (Oakville, Mo.); First Presbyterian Church (Myrtle Beach. S.C.); Manchester (Mo.) United Methodist Church; Trinity Presbyterian Church (University City, Mo.); Granite City (Ill.) Ministerial Alliance; Northeast and Northwest Associations, Wisconsin Conference, UCC; Ladue (Mo.) Chapel Presbyterian Church; Lafayette Park United Methodist Church (St. Louis, Mo.); Glendale (Mo.) Presbyterian Church; and Williamsburg (Va.) Presbyterian Church.

As always, many thanks to Eden Adminsitrative Assistant, Mary Swehla, who is better than a thousand computers as she so ably and efficiently word processes the manuscripts that I still produce the old-fashiolned way with pen and pad.

J. Clinton McCann, Jr.

Clint McCann and I hatched the idea for this book when we were together at the "Psalms and Practice" conference held at Austin Theological Seminary in May 1999. In fact, the book's introduction grew out of a paper Clint presented at the conference, and the nucleus of some of the material covered in chapters 2 through 5 (of which I was the principal writer) appeared in a paper I presented. The fruit of that conference has been published as *Psalms and Practice: Worship, Virtue and Authority,* edited by our host in Austin, Stephen Breck Reid (Liturgical Press, 2001).

Our admiration for and gratitude to Roland Murphy know no bounds. Father Murphy is for us the heroic examplar of the pastor-scholar (or scholar-pastor), as he effortlessly embodies the marriage of critical inquiry to love of Christ and the church. For his counsel, mentoring, and friendship we give thanks to God.

Like Clint, I should thank the various churches in which I've preached and spoken on the Psalms, but I will single out just one.

The Myers Park United Methodist Church in Charlotte invited me to teach a "Wonderful Wednesday" series on the Psalms back in 1985. A young woman, sitting on the back row, raised her hand, asked a question, and caught my eye. After class, Reverend Ron Hall, amateur matchmaker, introduced us; and a year later Lisa and I were married. She has sat through countless talks and sermons I've given and has read through everything I've written, with great patience and greater love.

I want to thank Peter Krentz, professor of classics at Davidson College, for his usual superb critique of the manuscript. My longtime friend and now colleague as minister of music and the arts on my staff, John-Palmer Smith, contributed much to my work on the Psalms and this volume, as did Kevin Turner, a bright young star in church music. My associates Andy Baxter and Karen Easter read portions of the manuscript. Our secretarial staff, Linda Turner, Terrie Stark, Cherry Stevens, and Karen Bright, performed their usual happy, excellent work on the administrative side of the project.

My sermons in this volume were part of a months-long series on the Psalms preached to my wonderful congregation, Davidson United Methodist Church. They always listen with intelligence and eagerness, for which I am thankful to God. The sermons appear in this book pretty much as preached, not dressed up much for literary craftsmanship. They bear the essential signs of orality, and even of being prepared in the midst of a hectic week, which as we all know is how preaching happens, or not at all.

James C. Howell

PART I

Preaching the Psalms: Why?

CHAPTER 1

An Invitation

The title of this book is plain and obvious, nothing metaphorical or clever. It's a book about preaching the Psalms. We believe the Psalms should be preached, that they can be preached, that the life of the church is impoverished if we do not attend to the Psalms in our proclamation of the Word of God. Hence, our title, *Preaching the Psalms.*

But for many clergy, there is nothing obvious about preaching the Psalms. Not often does a Psalm serve as a text for a sermon, and the reasons for this omission are varied. Christian preaching inevitably gravitates toward the New Testament, and even though publishers have for centuries printed handy editions of "The New Testament and Psalms," those Psalms are still in the Old Testament and are riddled with bulls and altars, pleas for vengeance, kings and priests, a passion for the temple—all the agenda we think the New Testament has left in the dust. Later in the book we will question this assumption.

Others who think about preaching, and some of the great practitioners of the craft are among their number, feel that the Psalms are for singing, not preaching. In their training, seminarians are not given much encouragement to preach the Psalms. Donald Gowan, for instance, suggests that while Psalms should be used in worship, they should remain "in their appropriate place," that "we ought to pray them and sing them rather than preach them."[1] And David Buttrick, in his great textbook called *Homiletic: Moves and Structures*, confesses to "an odd notion that psalms are for singing and not, primarily, for preaching."[2]

There is nothing odd about Buttrick's notion. In the liturgy, the Psalms function as a means of responding to Scripture. We certainly welcome the renewal of Psalms in worship and the varied ways they are nowadays being sung and chanted in varied traditions. But they may also be preached. The meaning and usefulness of a text are not limited to its original intent or use. Clearly by the end of the Old Testament era, Psalms were being collected, suggesting that the leadership of Israel's religious life conceived of a broader application of the entire batch of Psalms beyond their original deployment as liturgies or individual prayers. The resulting "Psalter" has the character of a hortatory or instructional book—something to which we will return in chapter 3.

We have to reckon with the fact that, through the long history of the church, Psalms most certainly *have* been preached to great effect, as we will see in the next chapter. The Psalms are very much a part of our canon of Scripture, a fair enough warrant for the preacher who would weave a sermon around a Psalm.

Narrative and Poetry

Another superficial difficulty that may bracket Psalms out of the preaching menu is the popularity of narrative theology and narrative preaching. For many, "narrative" has assumed a privileged position in theological conversation, and "storytelling" is very much in vogue. We could argue, as did Robert Alter, that many Psalms can "be thought of as incipient narrative."[3] Most certainly, all the Psalms imply a narrative, and many of them (such as 78 or 106) actually rehearse in episodic style Israel's grand narrative.

But the Psalms are poetry, and we need not try to squeeze them into a narrative mold so they might qualify as preaching fodder. Walter Brueggemann titled one of his books about proclamation *Finally Comes the Poet*, borrowing a noble line from Walt Whitman:

> After the seas are all cross'd, (as they seem already cross'd,)
> After the great captains and engineers have accomplish'd their
>   work,
> After the noble inventors, after the scientists, the chemist, the
>   geologist, ethnologist,
> Finally shall come the poet worthy of that name,
> The true son of God shall come singing his songs.[4]

Brueggemann argues that to address the whole issue of truth in our world "requires us to be *poets that speak against a prose world*."[5] We are like Bertrand Russell's "flatlanders," a two-dimensional people, trapped on the prosaic surface of a sequence of events that passes by us swiftly. If Brueggemann is right, that the "primary pastoral task is to voice the felt loss, indignation, and bewilderment that are among us,"[6] then the Psalms become more essential than ever in preaching. For it is in the laments, numerically the most conspicuous type of Psalm passed down to us, that loss and bewilderment are articulated, even screamed, yet not into some void, but into the very heart of God.

Scholarship and the Psalms

The very mention of "laments" may direct us to another difficulty. We suspect that a large number of pastors shy away from the Psalms because they are unsure what to do with them. In most introduction courses to the Old Testament, the Psalter gets perhaps one or two lectures; and only the more diligent pastors get a handle on the methodological tools that could breathe life into a Psalm for preaching. In the past century, scholarship has devised a cluster of helpful approaches to the Psalms: categorizing them form-critically by genre, unearthing liturgical settings, recognizing meter and structure, locating the supplicants sociologically. Psalm 8 ("When I look at thy heavens, the work of thy fingers" [RSV]) is a hymn, a soaring doxology, downright homiletical as it extols the grandeur of creation and its Creator. We know that when supplicants were in distress, the priest would hear the prayer and articulate an oracle, which explains why most of the pleas for help end with a word of praise (e.g., Psalm 6:9, "The LORD has heard my supplication; the LORD accepts my prayer"). When thanksgiving sacrifices were offered, the worshiper would turn to relatives and friends and tell a story (e.g., Psalm 66:15-16, "I will make an offering of bulls and goats. Come and hear, all you who fear God, and I will tell what he has done for me"). Sometimes these kinds of confessions of faith would evolve into self-contained poems, the "Psalms of trust," the beloved Psalm 23 being the prime example. Refrains, repeated throughout a Psalm, create something of a rhetorical cadence (e.g., Psalms 42-43, "Why are you cast down, O my soul? . . . Hope in God"), which in a manner evidenced in the African American tradition could be used to great effect in a sermon. We can pinpoint the desperate plight of the poor who cry out of their destitution (e.g., Psalm 73), and also the weighty responsibility of the most affluent in the land (e.g., Psalm 72, "May he [the king] defend the cause of the poor, . . . give deliverance to the needy"). Scholarship can help us poke around behind, beneath, and inside the Psalms (and in chapters 4 and 5 we will consider in more depth ways in which scholarly methodologies can provide the preacher with an angle on various Psalms), proving that Thomas Merton was right when he said that the Psalms "sum up the whole theology of the Old Testament,"[7] and that Martin Luther was on target when he said that the Psalter is like a little Bible in itself.[8]

At the same time, we may recall Karl Barth's warning: "How much trouble the Bible makes the poor research workers!"[9] The preacher may be humbled and at the same time liberated by the fact that for centuries the Psalms have been prayed by people who knew nothing of scholarship, people for whom the words of the Psalter were utterly familiar, people whose lives came to be interwoven with the life of God by means of these ancient prayers.

When we were in graduate school together at Duke, one of us was asked by the great Roman Catholic scholar Roland Murphy to serve as a teaching assistant for a seminary class on the Psalms. Not being well-versed in Psalms scholarship at the time, I asked him what I should read in preparation—expecting to be assigned a list of a dozen or more tomes by Gunkel, Mowinckel, Weiser, Kraus, and similar Hall of Famers. To my surprise, he said, "Start off by simply praying the Psalms. One in the morning, one in the evening." Relieved, I assumed it would be a breeze—until that same week I paid a visit to a classmate who had been hospitalized at Duke Medical Center once more in her terrible bout with cystic fibrosis. Through labored breathing, she asked for a favor. Since the hospital was on the way from my apartment to the Divinity School, would I stop on my way in and on my way home, and say a prayer with her?

Of course I was happy to. But then she added, "You could just read a Psalm, and that could be our prayer." And so it was in the year 1980 that I learned the Psalms at a hospital bedside with a young woman as she was ushered into heaven on the words of the saints.

Questions and Answers

While the Psalms pose some peculiar challenges, preaching is preaching; and the wisdom of the great exemplars and teachers of homiletics should be remembered and need not be rehearsed once more in these pages. We do want to reflect for a moment on the observations of Karl Barth, written only a few years after he had taken up the preaching task while in the parish: "I sought to find my way between the problem of human life on the one hand and the content of the Bible on the other."[10] Later in his brilliant *The Word of God and the Word of Man*, he continues: "What the people want to find out and thoroughly understand is, *Is it true?* And so they reach, not knowing what they do, toward the unprecedented possibility of praying, of reading the Bible, of speaking, hearing, and singing of God."[11] And then this: "The Bible has a somewhat uncanny way of bringing into the church situation its *own* new and tense and mighty *(mightier!) expectancy*. If the congregation brings to church the great *question* of human life and *seeks an answer* for it, the Bible contrariwise brings an *answer*, and *seeks* the *question* corresponding to this answer: it seeks questioning *people* who are eager to find and able to understand that its seeking of them is the very answer to their question."[12] His illustration of how this questioning and answering plays itself out? The Psalms.

Not surprisingly, then, Barth preached often from the Psalter. To anyone who wonders whether to preach on the Psalms, or to anyone who wonders how to preach on the Psalms, we have sermons from Barth and Bonhoeffer, Luther and Calvin, Augustine and Jerome, virtually every giant in the history of the church, which are both our warrant and our tutor in this enterprise.

CHAPTER 2

A Great Tradition of Preaching

During the years that the mighty tomes of his *Church Dogmatics* were appearing, Karl Barth exercised a little-known preaching ministry at the prison in Basel. It is said that some citizens toyed with the idea of committing a crime just so they could hear his sermons. He would preach, visit in the cells, and give out cigars. On his seventieth birthday, Barth went to the prison and spoke on Psalm 34:6. Three months later he returned, selecting Psalm 39:8 as his text; the sermon was a ringing call to hope, which is something altogether different from immediate comfort. On New Year's Eve, 1960, Barth, now in his mid-seventies, climbed into the prison pulpit, addressed them with his usual "Dear brothers and sisters," and began a homily on Psalm 31:15 with a personal anecdote:

> I once had a good friend. . . . At the New Year of 1956 . . . he preached . . . on this text: "My time is secure in your hands." It was a very warm, meaty sermon, stirring and alive. . . . It was also this man's last sermon: five days later, when he had returned to Paris, he died quite unexpectedly. How do I know that today's is not my last sermon, too?[1]

And then Barth reminded them all that "my time does not belong to me." At the end of time we will be asked what we did with our time. The good news is registered in the Psalm: "My time is secure in *your* hands. Not in the hands of a dark, unfeeling fate. . . . My time is not in the hands of any great or humble man either . . . And the most important thing: My time is not in my own hands. It is a real piece of good fortune that I am not left to my own resources."[2] Then he asks the seemingly simplistic, earthy question: "But does God have hands?" Barth's answer is that God's hands are his deeds, his works, his words, and above all, the hands of Christ.

They are the hands which he held outstretched when he called: "Come unto me, all you that labour and are heavy laden, and I will give you rest." They are the hands with which he blessed the children. They are the hands with which he touched the sick and healed them. They are the hands with which he broke the bread and shared it out to the five thousand in the desert place and then again to his disciples before his death. Finally and above all, they are his hands nailed to the cross. . . . These are the hands of God: the strong hands of a father, the good, soft, gentle hands of a mother, the faithful, helping hands of a friend, the gracious hands of God, in which our time is secure.[3]

We may ask questions about Barth's imaginative move from the Psalm to Christology, an issue we will probe later. But the power of the sermon cannot be denied.

Bonhoeffer and Niemöller

Let us look to another giant of the twentieth century. In the summer of 1928, Dietrich Bonhoeffer, a mere twenty-two-year-old, chose Psalm 62 as his text when he preached to the German congregation in Barcelona, where he was the assistant pastor.[4] He began by imploring the ancient Psalmist: "You appear to us like an image from a pleasant dream that we long for, yet find so distant from us. We are attracted to you, but we no longer understand you. Teach us something about the silence of the soul, the soul that waits for God." Next Bonhoeffer rings the changes on a cluster of images—thirst, heat, shadow, hurriedness, breathing, making space. His diagnosis of our perplexity is probing:

We are so afraid of silence that we chase ourselves from one event to the next in order not to have to spend a moment alone with ourselves, in order not to have to look at ourselves in the mirror . . . We are not only afraid of ourselves and of self-discovery, we are much more afraid of God—that he may disturb us and discover who we really are, that he may take us with him into his solitude and deal with us according to his will.

Bonhoeffer, anticipating the wise book he would write fifteen years later on the Psalms,[5] links this fearfulness to the way our "moods" determine our prayer. "We may regard religion as a matter of mood if we wish, but God is not determined by our moods; one does not wait until overtaken by a feeling to encounter him." Prayer is in fact "sober work and practice." We do not intuitively know how to pray; "we must learn the language of God . . . so that we will be able to speak to him." Perhaps this is a clue to how the Psalter functions as Scripture. A Psalm like 62 is God's word to us, exposing who we are, but also teaching us how to connect with God.

Bonhoeffer lost his life because of his courageous opposition to Hitler. A colleague who barely escaped with his life was Martin Niemöller. Among the last twenty-eight sermons Niemöller preached before his arrest, compiled and published as *God Is My Führer*, are two based on Psalm texts. For the evening service on April 7, 1937, he chose Psalm 94:16-22, "Who will rise up for me against the evildoers?" With Nazi shadows lengthening every day, engulfing Germany in darkness, that was a poignant question. Perhaps if good Christians had answered that question, the atrocities of Nazism could have been avoided. Not that battling evil is ever easy. Niemöller knew what he was talking about when he went on to say that disciples of Jesus must bear hatred, enmity, physical danger. For this reason, the balance of Psalm 94 ("thy mercy, O LORD, held me up . . . the LORD is my defense; and my God is the rock of my refuge") is precious to the preacher, for it speaks of comfort and solace in the face of persecution, how Christ himself was counted among those afflicted.

On New Year's, 1937, Psalm 92 served as Niemöller's text to prepare his congregation for an ominous year. His sermon is a warning against naïve optimism. For the gospel was being banished from public life; attacks were being launched on the confessing church. In the face of such depressing burdens, though, Christians are still called to engage in a happy work: "It is a good thing to give thanks unto the LORD!" (Psalm 92:1 KJV). The devil tempts us to focus only on our distress. It's all a matter of vision. Blind eyes see only a child in a stall, a suffering man on a cross.

> But the eyes that God has opened see in the child in the manger the only begotten Son of God and in the suffering man on the cross the Saviour of the whole world. . . . Yes, dear brethren; we have reason indeed to give thanks . . . Meanwhile, of course, we must be called fools and imbeciles, dreamers and visionaries. . . . for in the world, as we know, nothing counts but what is visible.[6]

Then, after reflecting on a catena of verses from Old and New Testaments about the power of God, he adds a rhetorical flourish, concluding with the fourth verse of Psalm 92: "If we believe Him, dear brethren, if we know that we are safe in His hands, how can we possibly be afraid, how can we possibly act as though He were not the Lord to Whom all power belongs in Heaven and on earth, how can we possibly not join in singing: 'Lord, Thou hast made me glad through Thy work: I will triumph in the works of Thy hands!'"[7]

Ten days after Niemöller was arrested, Bonhoeffer daringly preached on Psalm 58, one of the Psalms that expresses rage and seeks vengeance. While pronouncing judgment on the Nazis, the sermon urges peacefulness among Christians. Vengeance is God's business alone, not ours; Bonhoeffer was still two years from engaging in more pointed resistance to the Third Reich. He wound up the sermon with a theological flourish about Jesus Christ, who

> was stricken by God's wrath and vengeance. His blood is the blood which God's righteousness required. . . . Only he who bore the vengeance could pray for the forgiveness of the wicked. . . . Christ prays this Psalm as our representative. He accuses the wicked, he calls down upon them God's vengeance and his righteousness, and he gives himself for all the wicked in his innocent suffering on the cross.[8]

King and Luther

An innocent sufferer in America also preached from the Psalms. For Martin Luther King, Jr., as for hundreds of his colleagues, virtually every sermon gravitated toward Psalm 13:1 as its "real" text: "How long?" Richard Lischer, in his great book on King's preaching, alludes to a study by William Pipes suggesting that in the black church tradition, that plaintive query—"How long?"—is like touching a match to gasoline.[9] In a dizzying pulpit flourish in 1966, King took the ancient, familiar claim of Psalm 24:1 and pointed it straight at southern discrimination: "God has not yet decided to turn this world over to George Wallace. Somewhere I read, 'The earth is the Lord's and the fullness thereof.'"[10]

King's very name points us back to the beginning of the Protestant Reformation. Four days before Christmas in 1516, a very young Martin Luther preached on Psalm 19 and voiced a youthful but profound expression of the theology of the cross. Human glory is vanity; the works we do are nothing better than sins. God's "proper" work is to create righteousness, peace, mercy, truth, joy. But God "makes use of a greater disturbance," his "alien" work, by which God reveals our sin and pronounces us guilty. This alien work is the cross of Christ. The "law" praised in the Psalm "is an excellent thing, in so far as it points out sins and makes us realize our own misfortune, and thus moves us to seek the good."[11] That good is God's proper work, which is the resurrection of Christ.

Five years before he nailed his Ninety-five Theses on the Wittenberg door, and eight years before he declared "Here I stand!" at the Diet of Worms, Martin Luther developed a series of lectures on the book of Psalms that proved to be the turning point in his thinking. The text of the Psalms pressed him to understand the spirit of Scripture, the hiddenness of God, and our solidarity with Christ. For the rest of his life, he explained the Psalms, "not for Nuremburgers, that is, cultured and smart people, but for coarse Saxons, for whom Christian instruction cannot be chewed and prechewed enough even by my wordiness."[12]

In 1532 he wrote a little exposition of Psalm 147 because of a friend's hospitality on a hunting trip (and Luther actually refrained from the hunt, using the time to write the exposition!). In 1526 he interpreted four Psalms to ingratiate himself to Queen Mary of Hungary, whose anti-Reformation husband had just drowned. Not only did he preach directly from the Psalms constantly, but virtually every sermon on any text meanders before it is complete to some Psalm or another, usually his favorites, Psalms 51, 32, 117, 70, and 118 (which he called "an outstanding remedy for me against the plots and wiles of the devil. This is why I love it so and want to see it enriched and adorned with every possible device and figure of speech. . . . It is dearer to me than all the wealth, honor, and power of the pope, the Turk, and the emperor").[13]

Augustine and Jerome

As a Catholic, Luther belonged to an order named for the greatest theologian of the early church. Augustine, who preached sitting while the congregation stood, spoke extemporaneously and imaginatively on the Psalms to a relatively sophisticated congregation in Carthage just after the turn of the fifth century. Scribes hustled to get his words onto paper—and the combined results, the *Enarrationes in Psalmos*, became one of the major theological texts throughout the Middle Ages and into the Reformation. For Augustine, each Psalm mysteriously contained the entire Bible *in nuce*, and his expositions of the Psalms are marvels of theology and pastoral care.

When Augustine spoke to catechumens during their Lenten preparation for baptism, he focused on the "longing for flowing streams" in Psalm 42. At the celebration of the martyrs he preached on Psalm 70; the sufferings of the ancient poet stirred him to speak of the imitation of the passion of Christ by the blessed martyrs, who would indeed pray that their persecutors be "confounded" (v. 1), that is, "converted"—which in fact happened. "Kings believed, peace was given to the Church, the Church began to be set in the highest place of dignity, even on this earth."[14] On Good Friday he preached, naturally enough, on Psalm 22.

Turning to Psalm 23, Augustine began, "The Lord Jesus Christ is my Shepherd"; for him, the "still waters" represented baptism, and the "table" and "house of the Lord" were figurative of the Eucharist. And in a bold stroke, he expostulated as follows on the graphically violent final verse of Psalm 137, "Let her little ones be dashed": "What are the little ones of Babylon? Evil desires at their birth. For there are, who have to fight with inveterate lusts. When lust is born, before evil habit giveth it strength against thee, when lust is little, by no means let it gain the strength of evil habit; when it is little, dash it. Dash it against the Rock; and that Rock is Christ."[15]

Early in the fourth century, Augustine's contemporary, Jerome, had settled in to life as a monk in the village of Bethlehem—so as to be near the Lord's birthplace. His exploits ranged from translating the Hebrew Old Testament to pulling a thorn from a lion's paw. We have several dozen sermons he preached on the Psalms to other monks and pilgrims. Expounding Psalm 1, he said, "The Psalter is like a stately mansion that has only one key to the main entrance. Within the mansion, however, each separate chamber has its own key. Even though the great key to the grand entrance is the Holy Spirit, still each room without exception has its own smaller key."[16]

When preaching on Psalm 137 he turned the same key Augustine had. When the Psalm cries harshly for vengeance with the declamation, "Happy shall he be who takes your little ones and dashes them against the rock" (RSV), he spiritualized the text and suggested the little sins, before they grew up to be big sins, should be smashed on the Rock, which is either Christ, or else the church.

Jerome spoke on Psalm 132 and its mention of Bethlehem—their own home. If his fellow monks thought they endured discomforts, he points them to Christ.

> O monks, the Lord is born on earth, and He does not have even a cell in which to be born; there was no room for Him in the inn. The entire human race had a place, and the Lord about to be born had none. He found no room among men; He found no room in Plato, none in Aristotle, but in a manger, among beasts of burden and brute animals, and among the simple, too, and the innocent.[17]

The clefts in the rock, mentioned in Psalm 78, become for Jerome the wounds of Christ; the outstretched hands of Psalm 91 are those of the crucified Lord. The "new song" of Psalm 98 is that of the resurrection.

From St. Peter Through Modernity

Preaching from the Psalms can be observed further back in Christian history. Origen, reading in Psalm 90:14 that mercy comes "in the morning," concluded that this naturally signifies the resurrection of Christ. Peter's sermon in Acts 2 is woven out of Old Testament quotations, most of which come from the Psalms (he cites Psalms 16, 110, and 132). Indeed, Psalm 110:1 ("The LORD says to my lord, 'Sit at my right hand until I make your enemies your footstool'") is the most frequently quoted verse in the entire New Testament, and seems to have served as a springboard for the first Christians trying to comprehend the scope of Christ's work and significance.

But we may also move forward in time. Lancelot Andrewes (1555–1626), chaplain to both Tudor and Stuart courts, selected Psalm 77:20 ("Thou didst lead Thy people like sheep, by the hand of Moses and Aaron") as his text for a sermon preached before Queen Elizabeth at Greenwich on February 24, 1590. Andrewes, in a manner that may make today's preacher squirm a little, saw the rod of government as a divine gift. The preacher spoke of the burdens of ruling, and eloquently applied them to the queen herself: "It is surely supernatural to endure that cark and care which the governors continually do—a matter that we inferiors can little skill of. . . . Wherefore when we see that careful mind in a prince, I will use Moses' own words, to carry a people in her arms, as if she had conceived them in her womb, as no nurse, nor mother more tender . . . let us see God sensibly in it."[18]

On January 29, 1625, the dean of St. Paul's cathedral in London, the famous poet John Donne, began his sermon on Psalm 63:7 with the profession that "the Psalms are the manna of the church. As manna tasted to every man like that that he liked best, so do the Psalms minister instruction and satisfaction to every man in every emergency and occasion."[19] Donne's last sermon, titled "Death's Duel," preached as he was dying late in the winter of 1630, heard in person by Charles I, was based on Psalm 68:20 ("And unto God the Lord belong the issues of death"). Profoundly exploring our mortality, he turns his gaze to the one who became mortal for us, in whom we must trust. "There we leave you in that blessed dependency, to hang upon him that hangs upon the cross, there bathe in his tears, there suck at his wounds, and lie down in peace in his grave, till he vouchsafe you a resurrection, and an ascension into the Kingdom, which he has purchased for you with the inestimable price of his incorruptible blood."[20] And so ends Donne's last sermon, a final paean of praise on the lips of one who loved the Psalms, and who might have written a few himself.

Nineteen years later, King Charles was beheaded. In the aftermath of revolution, a man charged with regicide defended his action before Oliver Cromwell with the text of Psalm 149: "Bind your kings with chains, and your nobles with fetters of iron." John Milton, notorious in his own day as a political activist, suggested that this binding of kings in chains was "an honour belonging to his saints," undoing "those European kings which receive their power not from God but from the Beast."[21] Dr. Robert Jenison, required to preach a sermon to demonstrate his obedience, once having been suspected of Puritanism, began well but drifted into Psalm 33:16, "There is no king saved by the multitude of a host." Drawing fire, he remonstrated that he was only talking about

27

man's weakness without God.[22] Vavasor Powell preached on the right of the lower classes to rule, pointing to Psalm 113 as warrant. Peter Sterry, treating Psalm 18, suggested that "the earth often signifies the common people; the hills the potentates of the earth. . . . The foundations, the greatness of the potentates, are moved and taken away by these shakings of the earth. . . . Those evil spirits which rule us as the gods of this world clearly perceive the foundations of their kingdom to be shaken and almost overthrown."[23] George Cockayne, preaching to the House of Commons, focused on Psalm 82:7, "and fall like one of the princes." The Puritans loved the Old Testament as a whole, and found in its metaphors a program for action.

Spurgeon's *Treasury*

To many, pride of place in the history of preaching and in the treatment of the Psalms belongs to Charles Haddon Spurgeon (1834–92), who commanded the pulpit of the cavernous Metropolitan Tabernacle in London, constructed for the thousands who could not hear enough of him. In his *Treasury of David*, his *magnum opus* expounding the Psalms, he demonstrates his wise grasp on where the history of interpretation is located. Praising Psalm 90, he avers: "Many generations of mourners have listened to this Psalm when standing around the open grave, and have been consoled thereby, even when they have not perceived its special application to Israel in the wilderness."[24] Or considering Psalm 100: "It is all ablaze with grateful adoration, and has for this reason been a great favourite with the people of God ever since it was written. 'Let us sing the Old Hundredth' is one of the everyday expressions of the Christian church, and will be so while men exist whose hearts are loyal to the Great King."[25]

His treatment of Psalm 22, the Psalm Jesus voiced from the cross, is exemplary. "Before us we have a description both of the darkness and of the glory of the cross. . . . Oh for grace to draw near and see this great sight! We should read reverently, putting off our shoes from off our feet, as Moses did at the burning bush, for if there be holy ground anywhere in Scripture it is in this Psalm."[26]

Contemplating the cry of dereliction, "My God, my God, why hast thou forsaken me?" Spurgeon suggested that "the Jews mocked, but the angels adored when Jesus cried this exceeding bitter cry. . . . Let us gaze with holy wonder, and mark the flashes of light amid the awful darkness of that midday-midnight. First, our Lord's faith beams forth and deserved our reverent imitation; he keeps his hold upon his God with both hands and cries twice, 'My God, my God!' . . . Oh that we could imitate this cleaving to an afflicting God!" He continues: "For our prayers to appear to be unheard is no new trial, Jesus felt it before us. . . . No daylight is too glaring, and no midnight too dark to pray in; and no delay or apparent denial, however grievous, should tempt us to forbear from importunate pleading. . . . He knows too well his Father's goodness to let outward circumstances libel his character."[27]

Further into the Psalm we find verse 14, "I am poured out like water."

> He was utterly spent, like water poured upon the earth; his heart failed him, and had no more firmness in it than running water, and his whole being was made a sacrifice, like a libation poured out before the Lord. He had long been a fountain of tears; in Gethsemane his heart welled over in sweat, and on the cross he gushed forth with blood. . . . How every incident of Jesus' griefs is here stored up in the treasury of inspiration, and embalmed in the amber of sacred song.[28]

Spurgeon even manages an aside on a moral woe of his day: "It may be noted that the habit of gambling is of all others the most hardening, for men could practise it even at the cross-foot while besprinkled with the blood of the Crucified. No Christian will endure the rattle of the dice when he thinks of this."[29]

Preachers in America

American preachers have favored the Psalms. The second paragraph of Jonathan Edwards's famous sermon, "Sinners in the Hands of an Angry God," preached at Enfield on July 8, 1741, fingers Psalm 73:18 to strike holy fear into the hearts of sinners: "Surely thou didst set them in slippery places: thou castedst them down into destruction" (KJV).

Henry Ward Beecher preached at Plymouth Congregational Church in Brooklyn, New York. Just before the Civil War he preached on Psalm 23: "David has left no sweeter psalm than the short twenty-third." He called it "the nightingale of the psalms. It is small, of a homely feather, singing shyly out of obscurity; but O, it has filled the air of the world with melodious joy, greater than the heart can conceive. Blessed be the day on which that psalm was born. . . . It has poured balm and consolation into the heart of the sick, of captives in dungeons, of widows in their pinching griefs, of orphans in their loneliness. Dying soldiers have died easier as it was read to them."[30] Beecher's thoughts were published and reprinted many times; they were included in a book that came out in 1904, by William A. Knight (*The Song of Our Syrian Guest*), that remarkably sold two million copies. Leslie Weatherhead and many others quoted Beecher, and the Psalm stands today as our most beloved Psalm and one that even the timid preacher has attempted at a funeral or two.

The coffin bearing the body of Abraham Lincoln stopped in Philadelphia on its journey from Washington to Illinois. Phillips Brooks, rector of Church of the Holy Trinity (and the author of "O Little Town of Bethlehem"), sanctified the moment with a sermon on Psalm 78:71-73. The eloquent tribute compared Lincoln to King David:

> God brought him up as he brought David up from the sheepfolds to feed Jacob, his people, and Israel, his inheritance. He came up in earnestness and faith, and he goes back in triumph. As he pauses here today, and from his cold lips bids us bear witness how he has met the duty that was laid on him, what can we say out of our full hearts but this—" He fed them with a faithful and true heart, and ruled them prudently with all his power." The Shepherd of the People! that old name that the best rulers ever craved. What ruler ever won it like this dead President of ours? He fed us with counsel when we were in doubt, with inspiration when we sometimes faltered, with caution when we would be rash. . . . He fed hungry souls all over the country with sympathy and consolation. He spread before the whole land feasts of great duty and devotion and patriotism, on which the land grew strong. He fed us with solemn, solid truths. . . . He spread before us the love and fear of God just in that shape in which we need them most, and out of his faithful service of a higher Master who of us has not taken and eaten and grown strong? "He fed them with a faithful and true heart." Yes, till the last.[31]

The Twentieth Century

Many great sermons from our own day have emerged from the Psalms. Some deploy the intensely personal language of the Psalter to plumb the depths of our mental or spiritual state. Gardner Taylor, during more than four decades as pastor of Concord Baptist Church in Brooklyn, frequently took a Psalm as his text. In a sermon titled "Spiritual Success," Taylor imagined an "oldster" being asked how he lived to be a hundred years old. His saucy answer? "I believe I have lived as long as I have because I drink a jigger of gin every morning and have done so for sixty or seventy years." We want to be privy to secrets of success, perhaps especially in that ever elusive spiritual realm. Taylor wisely leads us into the heart of the eighth verse of Psalm 16:

> I venture the comment that there is nothing we do which is not aimed at satisfying us spiritually. The new car? It makes us feel successful. The new clothes? They give us a sense of well-being. So we keep searching, trying on, contracting, and changing. All of this is aimed at the person within. Now, here is a man who seems calm, poised, at peace with himself, radiant with faith, his face aglow with a light which comes from neither sea nor land. The reporters crowd in upon him: tell us how it is done. And he answers, "I have set the Lord always before me: because he is at my right hand, I shall not be moved."[32]

Still other preachers have glimpsed the political, even cosmic dimension to the Psalter. In 1994, Fleming Rutledge scanned her lectionary for Ascension Day and selected Psalm 47. In the pulpit of Manhattan's Grace Episcopal Church, she juxtaposed the hymnic refrains from ancient Israel ("God is king over all the earth. . . . The rulers of the earth belong to God") with a news flash from Pretoria, one relating the stunning shift of power from racist South Africans to men like Nelson Mandela, celebrated by men like Archbishop Desmond Tutu. When Jesus ascended, he queried the disciples: "Why are you looking up into heaven?" For the place to look for Jesus is here, now, on earth. What Rutledge saw through the press—a throng from Soweto dancing and singing the same songs of hope and courage that had been their promise for decades, the shocking gesture of Mandela clasping hands with his former foe, F. W. deKlerk, calling him "one of the greatest sons of our soil"—all confirmed the truth of the Psalm, and surely inviting us all, as the Psalm begins, to "clap your hands, all you peoples; shout to God . . . for the rulers of the earth belong to God."[33]

The Psalms have been preached, are preached, and will continue to be preached, and when we preach them, we step into that tradition, mirroring the image Bernard of Chartres drew of medieval thinkers as "pygmies on the shoulders of giants," humbly yet proudly joining that great chorus of witnesses in expounding the Psalter. The history of the interpretation of the Psalms teaches a second lesson as well, and that is that the Psalms are very much a part of Scripture, the inspired Word of God. The way we frame our understanding of the Psalms as Scripture may even help us understand in more depth other portions of the Bible as Scripture.

CHAPTER 3

A View of Scripture

The church has never bracketed the Psalms off in a separate category, as if the book were somehow not as "inspired," as if the book were not part of the revealed Word of God. In the early Church, Diodore of Tarsus († 390) opened his prologue to his commentary on the Psalms by citing 2 Timothy 3:16 ("All Scripture is inspired by God, and profitable for instruction, for reproof, for correction"): "One would not be mistaken in applying this whole encomium of Holy Scripture to the book of the holy Psalms. For it teaches righteousness gently and reasonably to those who wish to learn, it reproves the rash carefully and without roughness, and it corrects whatever unfortunate mistakes are made, either by accident or by our own choices."[1]

Often we hold in our minds a truncated view of Scripture, assuming that the Bible is a great pooling of oracles, lightning bolts from heaven, words spoken by God, or at least words that tell great things about who God is and what God has done. But not everything in the Bible can be squeezed into this mold; not everything is etched in stone, direct from the hands of God. Although not alone, the Psalter stands as proof that the Bible is not a monolithic revelation from God to us. A conversation is going on between God and the people of God; in an elusive yet marvelous gray area, a relationship unfolds between a God who is mighty but mysterious and real people who are full of faith and yet riddled with doubts and pain. Not everything about God has been or could be corralled into narrative alone. The canon incorporates numerous blocks of poetry, inviting us to grasp dimensions of God and the life of faith both imaginative and mundane, realistic and spiritual.

Scripture as Incarnational

We hold to an "incarnational" view of Scripture. Just as God entered into the mundane realities of our mortal life in the person of Jesus, yet was not diminished but only truly revealed in that embodiment, so it is with all of Scripture, and perhaps especially the Psalms. We have in the Psalms the darkest and the brightest of human words to and about God. And just as God can be known and extolled through shimmering words of praise, so God is also known precisely in the dungeons of despair and agony. The very heart of Jesus, after all, was exposed; and revelation was consummated at the moment of Jesus' wrenching cry from a Psalm: "My God, my God, why have you forsaken me?" (22:1)

Such a view of Scripture is scandalously particularistic, and far from tidy. But in our hearts we know that "only a suffering God can help" (Bonhoeffer). Only a revelation woven into the very fabric of real life can in fact be revelation for us mortals. Let us consider what some of the greatest Christian thinkers have said about the Psalter as Scripture.

Thomas Merton said that "the Psalms bring our hearts and minds into the presence of the living God."[2] Beautifully he notes how it happens that we apprehend God through the Psalms: "The Church indeed likes what is old, not because it is old but rather because it is 'young.' In the Psalms, we drink divine praise at its pure and stainless source, in all its primitive sincerity and perfection . . . for the Psalms are the songs of men who *knew who God was*. . . . For God has willed to make Himself known to us in the mystery of the Psalms."[3]

Mirror of the Soul

And we learn the truth about ourselves. Athanasius suggested that "these words become like a mirror to the person singing them, so that he might perceive himself and the emotions of his soul, and thus affected, he might recite them."[4] John Calvin called the Psalter "an anatomy of all the parts of the soul," for "there is not an emotion of which any one can be conscious that is not here represented as in a mirror. Or rather, the Holy Spirit has here drawn to the life all the griefs, sorrows, fears, doubts, hopes, cares, perplexities, in short, all the distracting emotions with which the minds of men are wont to be agitated."[5]

Later we may quarrel with Calvin in that our griefs, doubts, and hopes are not to be overcome as distractions to our life with God, but rather are the very windows through which we see the truth not merely about ourselves but also about God. Diodore understood this well, noting that as we sing Psalms daily or in worship, we may not realize their inspired nature until we are in situations when we need the Psalms. Then we find in them "a most useful medicine," because "the wound we then suffer almost physically forces the Psalm's real meaning upon us, and the medicine once again begins to fit and to contain the disease to which it corresponds."[6]

Martin Luther penned this familiar and eloquent introduction to the Psalter, which he called "a little Bible":

> Where does one find finer words of joy than in the Psalms of praise and thanksgiving? There you look into the hearts of all saints, as into fair and pleasant gardens, yes, as into heaven itself. There you see what fine and pleasant flowers of the heart spring up from all sorts of fair and happy thoughts toward God, because of his blessings. On the other hand, where do you find deeper, more sorrowful, more pitiful words of sadness than in the psalms of lamentation? There again you look into the hearts of all the saints, as into death, yes, as into hell itself. How gloomy and dark it is there, with all kinds of troubled forebodings about the wrath of God! So, too, when they speak of fear and hope, they use such words that no painter could so depict for you fear or hope, and no Cicero or other orator so portray them.[7]

Concluding, Luther construed a crucial turn for how we think of Psalms as Scripture: "And that they speak these words to God and with God . . . " The Psalms indeed begin as words *to* God. But as they have been gathered up into the life of the community, and as they found their place in the canon of Scripture, they become words we speak *with* God. We discover that these words *to* God become for us the Word *of* God. The old saying, *lex orandi, lex credendi,* is valid: the law of prayer is the law of belief; what we pray, we believe. As Calvin said of the Psalms, "In proportion to the proficiency which a man shall have attained in understanding them, will be his knowledge of the most important part of celestial doctrine."[8]

Subversive School

These are the prayers of people who lived millennia ago, to be sure. But Gerald Sheppard is right: "Strange as it may seem, Old Testament prayers were almost always meant to be overheard by others."[9] Indeed, as Christoph Barth put it, the Psalms are "a school of prayer." Bonhoeffer, as clouds of evil gathered over Europe in 1939, wrote,

> The phrase "learning to pray" sounds strange to us. If the heart does not overflow and begin to pray by itself, we say, it will never "learn" to pray. But it is a dangerous error, surely very wide-spread among Christians, to think that the heart can pray by itself. For then we confuse wishes, hopes, sighs, laments, rejoicings—all of which the heart can do by itself—with prayer. . . . Prayer does not mean simply to pour out one's heart. It means rather to find the way to God and to speak with him, whether the heart is full or empty.[10]

Bonhoeffer wisely illustrates this learning by an analogy. Children do not just know how to talk. Rather, "the child learns to speak because his father speaks to him. He learns the speech of his father."[11] So it is as we learn to pray. And the child must be shaped and molded in ways that may not suit the child's immediate desires.

> If we are to pray aright, perhaps it is quite necessary that we pray contrary to our own heart. Not what we want to pray is important, but what God wants us to pray. If we were dependent entirely on ourselves, we would probably pray only the fourth petition of the Lord's prayer. But God wants it otherwise. The richness of the Word of God ought to determine our prayer, not the poverty of our heart.[12]

Walter Brueggemann has helped us understand how the Psalms function in this contrariness as Scripture. We will say more about the subject in chapter 4, when we analyze the Psalter's imagery and its imaginative effects. For now we can notice with Brueggemann that

The Psalms not only propose and constitute a world; they intend also to unmake, deconstruct, and unmask other worlds which seduce and endanger. . . . In fact, they articulate a *counter-world*, offered as a subversive alternative to the dominant, easily available worlds that are ever present in and tempting for Israel. The dominant, easily available world endlessly seducing Israel is one-generational, devoid of covenanting, morally indifferent, monologically closed, and politically indifferent. These Psalms voice a counter-world that practices exactly what the dominant world resists and denies. In its liturgic recital over a long period of time, Israel regularly enacted and embraced this counter-world as its true home.[13]

Indeed, he is echoing those famous words of Erich Auerbach, who noted the Bible's "tyrannical" claim to truth: "Far from seeking, like Homer, merely to make us forget our own reality for a few hours, it seeks to overcome our reality: we are to fit our own life into its world, feel ourselves to be elements in its structure of universal history."[14] The Bible, Psalms included, presents the one true world into which we must fit ourselves.

Psalms as Torah

In recent years, many scholars have grasped how the Psalms function as Torah.[15] In its final form, the Psalter has the coherence of a catechism, instruction not only in prayer but in the one to whom we pray and the movements of that one in life and history. Although the approach to the Psalms as instruction dates back to and before Calvin,[16] we now see how the canonical shape of the Psalter yields clues, tipping us off that it is to be so read. "Torah Psalms," those whose subject is the law and obedience to its teaching, are scattered throughout the Psalter, and usually at decisive junctures. Psalm 1 heads the entire collection, and Psalms 73, 90, and 119 introduce major divisions within the Psalter. Structural questions notwithstanding, the sense the reader gets from the entire compilation is that it can function as a school of prayer, inciting subversive, prayerful thinking and living, as radical and comprehensive as the Torah itself.

We must not forget that the primal nuance of "Torah" is not a legalism that breeds self-righteousness. Torah rather means "the way," an adventure of following, an embodiment of God's salvation and holiness in real life, a life of joy. Psalm 19 portrays this "Torah-life" as sweeter than honey, more precious than gold, not a burden, but genuine freedom.

Natan Sharansky was a Soviet dissident, imprisoned in 1977 for advocating free speech and the right to emigrate from the Soviet Union. His ordeal in prison was intense; his hope was buoyed by a Hebrew Psalter his wife, Avital, had given him. When he was freed, the guards tried to confiscate the Psalter and restored it to his hands only after he lay down in the snow and refused to leave without it. For Sharansky, that Psalter was the foundation of his "spiritual independence against the kingdom of lies."[17]

When thinking of the Psalms as Scripture, we may wisely urge those to whom we preach to think of the Psalms under the category of "spiritual formation." Bonhoeffer described how this "priceless treasure" must be touched upon regularly.

> When read only occasionally, these prayers are too overwhelming in design and power and tend to turn us back to more palatable fare. But whoever has begun to pray the Psalter seriously and regularly will soon give a vacation to other little devotional prayers and say: "Ah, there is not the juice, the strength, the passion, the fire which I find in the Psalter. Anything else tastes too cold and too hard."[18]

In those last two sentences, Bonhoeffer was quoting Martin Luther! Cambridge theologian David Ford continues the thought: "The self that is formed through this discipline is one in community with others who have prayed and continue to pray the Psalms, and so learns the language of this large community. There is no question of being able, out of one's own experience, to identify with everything that is prayed. Essential to the learning is that we pray as a community."[19]

Praying with Christ

When Bonhoeffer, who of course was never freed as Sharansky was, wrote that in praying the Psalms we "find the way to God and to speak with him, whether the heart is full or empty," he added, "No man can do that by himself. For that he needs Jesus Christ. . . . If he takes us with him in his prayer, if we are privileged to pray along with him, if he lets us accompany him on his way to God and teaches us to pray, then we are free from the agony of prayerlessness."[20] When we pray the Psalms, we pray together with Jesus, who brought all of humanity's needs, joys, and hopes before God.

By wedding the words of the Psalter to Jesus, Bonhoeffer joins the great tradition of preachers and saints, from Augustine to Jerome to Luther to Calvin to Spurgeon. Their rationale, and ours, is this: For the Christian preacher, the Psalter is not just Old Testament, but part of a unified canon, Old and New Testaments— or simply, the Bible. How we "move" with a Psalm to talk about Christ or the church is an art, requiring great care and skill. But the move has its own biblical warrant. Among many instances in the New Testament we may choose the most common (and most puzzling). The most frequently quoted Old Testament passage in all the New Testament is from a Psalm. The mysterious verse, Psalm 110:1, was the focal point of early Christian efforts to talk about the divinity of Jesus, about his Lordship over their lives, and indeed, over all things. To us this kind of prooftexting seems contrived. But Richard Bauckham has rightly noticed this about the New Testament authors:

> Precisely at the points where they appreciate most fully the new identity of God in Jesus they are engaged in exegesis, in the process of bringing the texts of the Hebrew scriptures and the history of Jesus into mutually interpretative interplay. We misunderstand this process if we see it as an attempt, by reading Christology back into the texts, to pretend that actually nothing at all was unexpected. The first Christians knew better than we do that some of the key insights they found in Deutero-Isaiah had not been seen in Deutero-Isaiah before. But the work of creative exegesis enabled them to find consistency in the novelty. They appreciate the most radically new precisely in the process of understanding its continuity with the already revealed.[21]

The God prayed to in the Psalms was not inconsistent with the person of Jesus. In fact, Jesus embodied the depth of God's nature in such a singular way that the first Christian writers included Jesus in the monotheistic identity familiar to Judaism.[22] What more poignant demonstration of an incarnational view of Scripture could be had? For it was the Twenty-second Psalm that Jesus, at his darkest moment, at the moment of his paradoxical glorification, cried out in dereliction, a cry that continues to challenge theologians, sensing as they rightly do that the heart of our faith is somehow hidden in that Psalm passing Jesus' lips.[23]

A Teachable Spirit

For any of Scripture, including the Psalms, to do its work, for us to pray with the one who was crucified, we need an attitude, a humble posture, one beautifully described in the autobiographical passage in Calvin's introduction to his Psalms commentary. Of his own conversion the Genevan reformer said:

> At first, since I was too obstinately devoted to the superstitions of Popery to be easily extricated from so profound an abyss of mire, God by a sudden conversion, subdued and brought my mind to a teachable frame, which was more hardened in such matters than might have been expected from one at my early period of life. Having thus received some taste and knowledge of true godliness, I was immediately inflamed with so intense a desire to make progress therein, that although I did not altogether leave off other studies, I yet pursued them with less ardour.[24]

The Psalms portray what we in turn must inculcate in ourselves in order to understand them: humility, desire, godliness, and teachability (Calvin's Latin is *dociliatem*, or "docile"). The preacher must grapple with the nemesis of an unteachability with which worshipers are infected during the week. Quick to "agree" or "disagree" with anything said, people do not raise docile antennae to absorb the Word of God. Everybody is a theologian, with bastions of defensive thoughts that shield the person from hearing the sermon and learning to pray with Christ. Our only hope is to remember that those defense works only appear to be formidable. In fact they are flimsy, a house of cards, and hearers may be caught unawares and discover the way to God quite by surprise.

To imagine what this may look like for preachers, and for those to whom they preach, let us recall the discovery of the Psalm scroll at Qumran. A young Bedouin shepherd named Jum'a Muhammad Khalil was passing the time by tossing stones into cave openings in the cliff. Something shattered inside. By chance he had hit upon a clay jar; and then he and a friend found several jars, full of the most spectacular manuscripts ever found. That was in 1947. Over the next five years the discoveries came quickly. But progress slowed. From 1953 to the end of 1955, very little was unearthed; and the sense was that the scroll finds were exhausted. Again it was not an archaeologist but a Bedouin who accidentally stumbled upon Qumran's Cave 11, featuring a marvelous Psalms scroll, fascinating us with its Psalm 151 and deviant ordering of all the Psalms. Most poignantly, in that scroll we can look at a community's prayer book from two millennia ago.

Hearing and preaching the Psalms may be like that. We search, we listen, we wait, for surprises, for some unexpected word from some unexpected quarter. Ultimately, the preacher must rely on the movement of the Spirit of God for the Word to be heard and to have its effects. Thomas Merton understood the role the Holy Spirit plays in the Psalms: "He, if you like, is the poet. But He also is the poetry. Or rather Christ, Whose Spirit He is, is the poetry of the Psalms. But the Holy Spirit, besides being the artist, is also the spectator. He is at the same time the poet, the poetry and the reader of the poetry."[25]

Consider the following sermon on Psalm 85, the text that St. Augustine interestingly had chosen to be read each year on Christmas Day. We offer this and other sermons throughout the book as real sermons preached in real churches on Psalms. "The Kiss" is a sample of treating a Psalm as Scripture, and also as an introductory example of our next subject: how to preach a Psalm, and especially its deployment of metaphorical language.

The Kiss: A Sermon on Psalm 85

Psalm 85 is a prayer that the Israelites prayed not just for themselves as individual people but also for the life of the community in which they found themselves.[26] They were in dire straits. They prayed for God to intervene, and then in their imaginations they began to think what it would be like when God's grace actually had done its work on their lives as individuals and on their community. The way they expressed that is, I think, one of the most remarkable bits of poetry that emanate from the Bible. In verse 10 of Psalm 85 they imagine that when the Lord acts, "steadfast love and faithfulness will meet," that "righteousness and peace will kiss each other."

Virtues: righteousness, peace, steadfast love, faithfulness. Unfortunately, we live in a world where virtues have fallen on hard times. They are not nearly as admired as success and pleasure, which seem to be what really drive us. There's a great moment in Mark Helprin's novel *Winter's Tale*, where a father tells his son the most important thing that he needs to tell his son. He says the virtues honesty, courage, sacrifice, and patience

> are never properly valued until one must lose a great deal for their sake and then they rise like the sun. Little men spend their days in pursuit of wealth, fame, and possessions. I know from experience that at the moment of their death they see their lives shattered before them like glass. Not so the man who knows the virtues and lives by them. The world goes this way and that. Ideals are in fashion or not, but it doesn't matter. The virtues remain uncorrupted, and uncorruptible. They are rewards in themselves. The bulwarks with which we can protect our vision of beauty.[27]

The Psalm says that these virtues meet, and that they kiss each other. Too often we see them as being separate. In our culture, we hope love and faithfulness coincide, but too often love flares up where there is no faithfulness at all and another marriage is lost. Or, back during the Reagan administration it seemed that the lesson that we were taught, that seemed difficult to argue with, was that at least in our world peace and righteousness do not easily go together. You had the Ollie Norths of the world who said that if you are righteous, you cannot have peace. You can only have peace by force and by violence and by deceit. The Psalm says that when the Lord comes, steadfast love and faithfulness will meet.

Righteousness and peace will kiss each other. I want to talk about kissing this morning. I like kissing. I don't know if you remember your first kiss. I don't know if you can remember your last kiss. Kissing is in something of an eclipse, having fallen on hard times, for a couple of reasons. One, we now have an atmosphere in which there is such a thing as sexual harassment. Early in my ministry that wasn't such a big deal. In my first parish there were a lot of women in church, most over eighty years old. They would kiss me leaving church—but now everyone is hesitant to touch because something might be misconstrued. The other reason that kissing has fallen on hard times, though, is that no one values the mere kiss anymore. It has been demoted and is now treated as a mere prelude toward the real thing.

A kiss. I remember my *nearly* first kiss with a girl. I was at one of those crazy parties in the seventh grade. As I look back on it, and my memory is foggy on this, we were at somebody's house. . . . Were the parents in another part of the house? Or had the parents relegated the house to a bunch of seventh graders for the night? I don't know. But we were playing some game, and somehow in the course of the game you drew lots. A boy and a girl were sent into this bedroom, into this walk-in closet. They closed the door. They were supposed to go in there and kiss. As the game was proceeding, my heart was just pounding—and I found myself becoming a holy man. I was praying, intently, that my time didn't come. Kids were going in and coming out. They were blushing and giggling, and I was thinking, "Oh, God"—and then finally it fell to me and little Marcie Estes. They compelled us to go into this closet. We went in there, and I was so relieved at first when Marcie came up with a brilliant suggestion. She said, "Let's don't kiss, let's just go out and pretend that we did." I thought, "This is great, yes!" We came out, and kind of giggled—and of course later I was a little bit wounded. Why didn't Marcie seize her opportunity? A couple of years later I was at Camp Kanuga up near Hendersonville. There was a girl there named Laurie. I kissed her, and she kissed back. It was great! Unfortunately she was from Colorado.

Kissing. You kiss different people and it means different things. I kiss my wife; I kiss my children. I remember as a little boy being kissed by my father—a pretty macho kind of guy. I must have been four or five, because after a while boys don't kiss because that's not a guy thing. But when I was a real little boy we did. My dad would go on these long, long trips; and when he would return home, we were so glad. He would come to the door; and he would pick me up; and there would be this combination hug, kiss, and noise, "Ummmmh!" I always thought there were air pockets under his skin. I do it to my kids now. I pick them up. Ummmmh!!

I was at a wedding yesterday. We heard the priest say, "You may kiss the bride." A kiss, it's a beautiful thing. It's an awesome thing. It doesn't suggest possessiveness. It's not even really something you do to get a whole lot of pleasure yourself. You kiss someone because you hold them in a very high regard. You value them, and you're saying through the kiss, "You matter, I care about you, there's a beauty about you." It's a beautiful thing, the kiss.

What it's about was put in front of me in the tenth grade. My English class had to read *Romeo and Juliet*—and it was lost on me at that stage. But listen: Juliet is up on the balcony and Romeo is beneath. He sees her and he says, "But soft! what light through yonder window breaks? It is the east, and Juliet is the sun." He talks about the brightness of her cheek—that it would shame even the beauty of the stars. He watches her a little longer, and then says, "See, how she leans her cheek upon her hand!/ O, that I were a glove upon that hand/ that I might touch that cheek."[28]

A kiss—a thing of beauty. In the Psalm the kiss is not between people. It is between what seems to us to be mere words: righteousness, peace, steadfast love, faithfulness. But the suggestion is that if they can meet and embrace and kiss, they are not mere ideas. They actually take on flesh and blood. They have a reality, a tangibility about them.

And when righteousness and peace kiss, it is a thing of beauty. Now what is beautiful? You and I know beauty when we see it. I remember I went to the Charlotte Coliseum a while back. I was sitting in my seat for some time. Finally I looked down to my left and there was this woman—and her beauty took my breath away. Now, she was short, and her shoulders were hunched over, and her skin looked just like sandpaper. She spoke with a thick accent. She was from Albania, but she spent most of her life in Calcutta. Mother Teresa combined righteousness and love and peace—and it was a thing of beauty.

Seven years ago our church's youth group went to Hatteras Island. A little mission building trip, sounds like fun—going to the beach. They went to the beach, and they repaired a porch that had been damaged in a hurricane. They nailed and hammered on a porch in front of somebody's house. Just somebody's house, nobody in particular. But then five years later, our associate pastor, who at the time was neither a reverend nor did he have any connection to Davidson United Methodist Church, went to Hatteras Island and asked to be paired up with somebody who was needy. They assigned him to Norma, who is the woman who lives in the very house that our youth group had built the porch for. He met Norma, and she's now dying. He told us about it last week. This week a lot of you sent her cards and letters. It's the kiss of righteousness and peace. A thing of beauty.

I went to Italy in late July. On my previous trip to Italy I visited a city halfway between Rome and Florence. In that city I went into a church and I saw a fresco—a real funny-looking guy. He was kind of short, and he had one hand reaching up toward God and another hand reaching down toward the poor. He'd grown up as a wealthy young man, a troubadour, a knight; but he had decided that his calling was to be a saint. And Francis of Assisi embodied for us what it means to say, "Lord, make me an instrument of your peace." We have Mission Day coming up on October tenth, and we hope that all of you will come out and serve on mission projects. I can't think of a better advertisement than this: Last year a man and a woman signed up for a project. They came and they looked at each other and thought, *He's/she's cute.* They are getting married soon. Think what can happen. The kiss of righteousness and peace.

We have a married couple who started coming to our church about a year ago. They said, "We have tried everything else. Our marriage is just terrible, and we thought it can't hurt too much just to give God a try; everything else has failed." They made God the center of their home. They're together, and they even tell me that the romance has returned.

There's a woman in our church, and she's got more kids than I do. Instead of her saying, "I've got all these kids. I'm up to my ears, and I just can't make any commitments. What am I going to do with all these kids?" Instead of that, if you go to a local retirement home, her name is on the wall more than once for being the volunteer of the month.

I was at a bookstore in Charlotte a while back, and I bumped into a guy there. I knew him, but he didn't know me. You would recognize him. He has one of those familiar faces that when you see it you say, "Ahhh." He's retired now, and it's interesting: In his retirement, instead of doing what, sadly, I think a lot of retirees do, saying, "I'm retired now; I can't make any commitments. That's for the young people. I'm enjoying my freedom now. I'm enjoying all those things that I worked for all those years." Instead of doing that he is spending all of his time working on righteousness and peace, building Habitat houses—and his name is President Jimmy Carter. The kiss of righteousness and peace. It is a thing of beauty.

I was at a party up in Bridgeport a few weeks ago. I met a married couple there. I talked to them a while. They seemed like normal folks. Their marriage was failing, by the way, back in 1965. The wife was seeing another man on the side. Her husband had no clue. He was making a million dollars a year and was absorbed in his work. He never noticed that he was losing his wife. She announced one day that she was going to leave him—that their marriage . . . there was nothing there. This made him panic. So he said, "Let's get in the car and take a vacation. Let's go down to Florida." On the way to Florida they stopped in Georgia to visit a friend. The friend said, "There's a Baptist preacher I want you to have lunch with." They had lunch with the Baptist preacher who turned out to be Clarence Jordan, and the rich man turned out to be Millard Fuller. He took his money and gave it away, but used his genius and brilliance and business sense to build over a hundred thousand homes to change lives and communities all around the world. The kiss of righteousness and peace. It is a thing of beauty.

But do you know what happens to you and me? We miss out on this kiss, and the reason we miss it is that you and I do what Marcie Estes and I did at that seventh-grade party. We go into our closets somewhere, when it comes to our faith, and we negotiate. We work out a little deal with ourselves. And the deal is, "Let's don't really kiss; let's just come out and pretend." We do it really well. We come to church, we smile, and say, "I'm a member of Davidson Methodist." Great church, great music. "I'm a Christian." And it's pretending. Our lives remain hollow until we go back into that closet and say, "Lord, I'm through pretending. I'm ready to be serious. I want love, faith, righteousness, peace."

I've asked you to do this before. Pull out your most clever, innovative imagination. Start to think of yourself as a person of righteousness and love and faithfulness and peace. Imagine that you get up in the morning and you do good all day long. Just at every turn you show love, and you make peace, and you exercise faithfulness, and you try to be righteous. You go at it all day long, and you get on a roll with it. The more you do it, the more natural it feels; and it begins to fit like an old glove. You do good all day long. You get ready to go to bed at night, and you don't really have any regrets at the end of the day. You think, "Life cannot get any better than this." Then you wake up the next morning and it does. That life of righteousness and peace: It just clings to you like a glove. And when you do that, you will discover when you wear that glove that your hand becomes the hand of Christ—and it is at that moment reaching up and touching the very face of God. Steadfast love and faithfulness will meet. Righteousness and peace will kiss each other. It is a beautiful thing.

PART II

Preaching the Psalms: How?

CHAPTER 4

The Exploration of Imagery

There is no one way to preach a Psalm. Just as we find a wonderful variety of Psalms within the Psalter, so we are invited to take varied approaches to the Psalms, and even to take varied approaches to the same Psalm.

Perhaps the easiest entry point to a Psalm for the preacher or for the reader is by way of an image. The Psalter exhibits a wealth of images, metaphors, figures; and they appeal not primarily to our rationality but to our imagination. We could fill a thick tome analyzing images from the Psalms: a despised worm, a nesting stork, a war horse, packs of dogs, sheep grazing, a watchman, a refiner, wings, the dew, winnowing, skin bottles, the volcano, hail, flowers, a thundercloud, a stone fortress, a deer sniffing the air for water. Each is like a still life. We take our watches off, and then we examine the color, we weigh the density, we listen for the breeze, we follow the scent, we savor the wine's aftertaste.

Each still life appeals to the imagination. Creation is not measured by its remoteness (15 billion years ago) or its force (the energy of the sun or its gravitational pull). Rather, the grandeur of creation is beyond science; and our theological articulation of the wonder of creation requires colorful, even mythic language: "You broke the heads of the dragons in the waters" (74:13). God is robed in light. . . . The clouds are God's chariot (104:1-3). God gathered as in a bottle the waters of the sea (33:7).

Every sermon must be attentive to these word pictures. If the preacher is tone-deaf or color-blind to word pictures, the sermon will plod about, flat-footed, and fail to draw the listener into the heart and spirituality of the Psalmist. If the Psalms teach us to pray, then people's spirituality can be expanded by learning to explore metaphorical language. Spurgeon was the master, both at plumbing the depths of biblical imagery and at devising his own variations upon the theme. Psalm 104:2 speaks of light as God's garment, prompting Spurgeon to imagine a monarch putting on his robe: "The conception is sublime: but it makes us feel how altogether inconceivable the personal glory of the Lord must be; if light itself is but his garment and veil, what must be the blazing splendour of his own essential being!"[1] Probing Psalm 6, Spurgeon rhapsodizes:

> Weeping is the eloquence of sorrow. It is an unstammering orator, needing no interpreter, but understood of all. Is it not sweet to believe that our tears are understood even when words fail! Let us learn to think of tears as liquid prayers, and of weeping as a constant dropping of importunate intercession which will wear its way right surely into the very heart of mercy, despite the stony difficulties which obstruct the way.[2]

Gerald Kennedy, who became a Methodist bishop in 1948, preached on Psalm 90 ("Before the mountains were brought forth . . . from everlasting to everlasting you are God"), and opened his sermon by telling of a young Welshman who walked through the Grand Canyon.[3] During the two-month trek, recounted in *The Man Who Walked Through Time*, this Welshman contemplated the scope of creation and the fading of millennia. The appropriateness of this image for this Psalm cannot be underestimated. Psalm 90 invites us to consider all things from that long, seemingly endless perspective of God's immense gaze over time. What Kennedy left unmentioned was that the Psalm compares God to a "dwelling place," and there are in the Grand Canyon nooks and crannies in those historic walls that shelter birds, just as we find very personal and sorely needed shelter in the God of time and space. Spurgeon sensed this nuance, and stepped into a great tradition of preaching on this theme, begun in the Middle Ages: "The clefts of the Rock of Ages are safe abodes."[4] Hear him ramble through Scriptures and history itself on Psalm 90:

> Moses, in effect says—wanderers though we be in the howling wilderness, yet we find a home in thee, even as our forefathers did when they came out of Ur of the Chaldees and dwelt in tents among the Canaanites. To the saints the Lord Jehovah, the self-existent God, stands instead of mansion and rooftree; he shelters, comforts, protects, preserves, and cherishes all his own. Foxes have holes and the birds of the air have nests, but the saints dwell

in their God. . . . We have not shifted our abode. King's palaces have vanished beneath the crumbling hand of time. . . . Go to the Palatine and see how the Caesars are forgotten of the halls which echoed in their despotic mandates . . . and then look upward and see in the ever-living Jehovah the divine home of the faithful, untouched by so much as the finger of decay. Where dwelt our fathers, a hundred generations since, there dwell we still.[5]

From Augustine to Generation X

You may trust that people sitting in the congregation are fascinated by images, given the explosion of symbolism in our media culture. Tom Beaudoin suggests that "any GenX pop culture interpretation is a chain of signs, with one image leading to another. . . . My task as a GenX theologian is to plumb, inquire, interrogate, associate, unleash, be playful, and look for traces of theological residue on the surfaces of these images."[6]

But the impulse to explore and discover ourselves and God through symbols is hardly novel. In *de doctrina Christiana*, St. Augustine gave classical definition to the way signs convey truth about God, the very presence of God. Many symbols are obscure or ambiguous; but "this situation was provided by God to conquer pride by work and to combat disdain in our minds, to which those things which are easily discovered seem frequently to become worthless."[7]

God is apprehended, not finally through scientific, rational, controllable categories, but by way of the imagination, a point well understood in recent theology. Garrett Greene makes an important clarification:

> Imagination turns out to be not the opposite of reality but rather the means by which manifold forms of both reality and illusion are mediated to us. Religions characteristically employ this power of imagination in order to make accessible the ultimate "shape," the organizing pattern, of reality itself, thereby illuminating the meaning and value of human life.[8]

Faith, or however we conceive of connecting with the things of God, is a daring act of the imagination, as our minds are stretched beyond the prosaic, around all we perceive, and thereby we discover that we are embraced by grace.

Images reveal, but images also conceal. Actually, images reveal by concealing. Or, as T. S. Eliot shrewdly suggested, "The chief use of the 'meaning' of a poem, in the ordinary sense, may be (for here again I am speaking of some kinds of poetry and not all) to satisfy one habit of the reader, to keep his mind diverted and quiet, while the poem does its work upon him: much as the imaginary burglar is always provided with a bit of nice meat for the house-dog."[9]

Hyperbole and the Soul

The Psalms are poetry.[10] Poetry is not just a decorative, artsy way of saying what could be said by prose. Rather, human experience is never merely prosaic and can never be fully captured in any narrative that measures time and place. Something in us stretches toward transcending that plane of cause and effect. There is a poet in each one of us, and there is poetry in the universe. The imagery in the Psalter is extravagant, hyperbolic, wildly flying about with exaggerations and overstatement. But the powerful image prods our memory, sweeps away the dust of the daily routine, seduces us into discovering and even expressing something we dared not face, or did not know how to face.

So we dare not "clean up" any image, no matter how offensive. Consider Psalm 137:9, "Happy shall they be who take your little ones and dash them against the rock!" Preaching on this text, Jerome sheltered the sensitive ears of his listeners, the monks who lived adjacent to the basilica in Bethlehem. Uneasy with such a scream for vengeance, he expounded the spiritual value of smashing tiny little sins before they grow into lethal ones.[11] The prayer evokes a fury long bottled up among the Israelites and can do so for modern people as well. Even Spurgeon understood the purgative effects of Psalm 137 and why we should not shudder at its horrific rage: "Let those find fault with it who have never seen their Temple burned, their city ruined, their wives ravished, and their children slain; they might not, perhaps, be quite so velvet-mouthed if they had suffered after this fashion."[12]

We dare not reduce the potential of an image to "what the original Psalmist intended." The poet Rainer Maria Rilke said that if you spend time with a book, you may discover ten times more meaning than was actually expressed by the original author.[13] Your own baggage and memories and cravings are read along with the words. This is how God uses Scripture. No doubt, some individual wrote each Psalm. But hear this wise evaluation from James Mays:

> There is an individual *in* each Psalm, known through the first person voice. . . . But the individual *in* the Psalm is not the same as the individual for whom the prayer was composed. The connection is not autobiographical or historical. The individual in the Psalm is an instance of a type . . . , a paradigm of the one who in trouble cries out to God for deliverance. The identity in the Psalm is given to and assumed by the one who prays the prayer. The language of the prayer is disclosive. It brings to light who one must be and who one is in crying out to the Lord from the depths of existence. It is this vagueness that frustrates explanatory questions, but it is also just this paradigmatic openness of the individual in the prayers that has made them so accessible for the praying of any and many. Down through the ages many have said they found themselves and their feelings and circumstances *in* these prayers. One comes to know liturgically and theologically who we are and what we need and one finds language to say it all to God.[14]

The fantastic images in the Psalms are not merely vehicles to say better what we already know and feel. An image may instead evoke some inner plight that had not previously been noticed; the image then works like an archaeologist, poking, digging about, brushing away layers of dirt accumulated over time until—well look! A broken pot. If we can find the shards scattered about and piece it all back together, it is a beautiful pot.

The accumulated dirt is not entirely psychological in nature. Our society and even the church itself have heaped dirt on the realities, the lives of every person to whom you preach. Brueggemann put it well:

> Whether this speech articulates, illuminates, or evokes experience, it does move the awareness and imagination of the speaker away from life well-ordered into an arena of terror, raggedness, and hurt. In some sense this speech is a visceral release of the realities and imagination that have been censored, denied, or held in

check by the dominant claims of society. For that reason, it does not surprise us that these Psalms tend to hyperbole, vivid imagery, and statement that offend "proper" and civil religious sensitivities. They are a means of *expressing* that tries to match *experience*, that also does not fit with religious sensitivity.[15]

The preacher can unfurl a Psalm and liberate worshipers from decades of pretending, inviting them through a biblical image or metaphor to discover the depths of their being, the heart of history, and thereby to discover God, or rather, finally realize that down in the guts of those unvisited sorrows, God is and has been and will be there. In Susan Howatch's novel, *Absolute Truths*, Charles Ashworth wisely says, "It occurred to me . . . that hell was not, as Sartre had proclaimed, other people. Hell was being obliged to pretend to be someone quite other than one's true self."[16] We shall say more about the healing that comes from this realization later in this chapter.

So each metaphor begs the reader to climb inside and try the image on for size. God invites us to explore the Psalter's images; God even trusts us to do so. The permutations available to the preacher therefore are innumerable. Psalm 130 begins, "Out of the depths I cry to you, O LORD." Leslie Brandt rendered the Psalms into modern categories back in the 1970s, and revised his reading in the late 1990s; in this Psalm he read the "depths" as follows:

> O God,
> Tonight I seek You with a heart full of guilt
> and a mind full of bewilderment and frustration.[17]

Similarly, dealing with a kindred text (Psalm 142:7, "bring my soul out of prison"), Halford Luccock hears "a cry from the dungeon of our animal inheritance," that "we are dungeoned by possessions, smothered by a clutter of merchandise, the life flattened out by the accumulative instinct of selfishness. The prison house of selfishness is the common jail of mankind, caging men in the little cell of personal advantage."[18]

But at about the same time Brandt was hearing "depths" as psychic darkness, Ernesto Cardenal, the Nicaraguan priest and political activist, gave us something more harsh to consider, a literal dungeon:

> From the depths, I cry to you oh Lord!
> I cry in the night from the prison cell
> and from the concentration camp
> From the torture chamber
> in the hour of darkness
> hear my voice
> my S.O.S.[19]

The absence of specificity in the text is the key to unlocking its applicability to all of God's people, and to the availability therefore of God's grace to all people. Had the text said, "Out of a prison cell in Asia I cry," that would shut out middle-class ennui, which seems pale compared to the experience of Cardenal, but is no less a condition to be offered up to God. Recently one of us met with a couple who had suffered the death of their infant son. Flailing about in his grief, the father could only find these words: "It just feels bottomless." We opened the Bible to Psalm 130, and the Psalm mercifully named their depths, and in so doing placed a firm floor beneath their feet so they might begin, however falteringly, to stand up, and wait, and hope once again.

Models and Permits

The Psalter's language is daring, bold, and imaginative—and the sermon can be no less so. Brueggemann argues that the Psalms are

> both models and permits. We stand under their discipline, and we are authorized by their freedom. In this movement *out of* the Psalms and then back *into* them, we are speakers for ourselves. We are at the same time speakers through countless generations, continuing the prayers and the speech begun for us long before us.[20]

Images most certainly break open our imaginations. The preacher daringly makes this movement in and out of the Psalm, and with some reckless abandon makes bold brushstrokes in the sermon. For the images of the Psalm partly express the emotions we know, but partly shape our mental life in unforeseen directions.

The preacher must never forget that the listener's experience may carry a kind of ambiguity that bears correction or reshaping.

Nicholas Lash put it well: "Our experience of God is by no means necessarily 'religious' in character nor, from the fact that a particular type of experience is appropriately characterized as 'religious,' may it be inferred that it is, in any special or privileged sense, experience of God."[21] We need to help people distinguish their feelings and experiences from knowing God, a distinction that requires some uncoupling and then reconnecting. For the Psalms are not just expressive of a heart pointed toward God. The Psalms are also constitutive: they shape our thinking by constructing a theological world that underlies and impinges upon the prosaic world we usually perceive, offering a critique of that reality and an invitation to be set free from that reality.

Robert McCracken, who was pastor of Riverside Church in New York City from 1946 to 1967, began a superb sermon on Psalm 42:11 with a terrific quotation by Alan Paton.[22] When asked what lay ahead for South Africa, Paton admitted that he did not know, that things might never change, that apartheid would grow more severe. So should we give up? leave? or stay the course?

> Stand firm by what you believe, do not tax yourself beyond endurance, yet calculate clearly and coldly how much endurance you have. Don't waste your breath and corrupt your character by cursing your rulers. Don't become obsessed by them, keep your friendships alive and warm, especially those with people of other races. Beware of melancholy, and resist it actively if it assails you.

The beauty of this opening is that it lifts the Psalmist's despair out of what could easily become for comfortable Americans an exercise in self-absorption. So the image is not just that the Psalmist is in despair, and the appropriate question therefore is not merely, "What is my own personal despair?" Rather, the image prompts now a broader question: "Who else is in despair?" Simply posing the question has some curative effect.

As is the case with Cardenal's S.O.S. from the prison cell, the language of the Psalter does not exist merely to name the hurt or anxiety that worshipers already bear in their guts. The Twenty-third Psalm is America's favorite, and our hearing of it hums with idyllic tones of sweetness and comfort. The preacher may help it to be heard in more depth by transporting the location of its reading elsewhere. Martin Niemöller, preaching in the Dachau concentration camp on Christmas Eve 1944, punctuated a sermon on Luke 2 with a quotation from Psalm 23: "You need not go to search for God; you should not imagine that He is far from you. . . . He is here and is close to you. . . . Whoever can grasp this in faith is not forsaken in prison and in death; for in the worst darkness he may say, 'Thou art with me; thy rod and thy staff they comfort me.'"[23]

The Psalms, if preached well, can draw us out of our own corner of suffering into an awareness of the broader suffering of others. Many Psalms are prayers from the lips of those who are impoverished. The exact identity of these "poor" is debated among scholars; the Hebrew word *anawim* admits of varying interpretations. But as preachers explore the theme of poverty in the Psalms, we dare not trivialize poverty into the sorry state of the modern psyche. A sermon may well invite a congregation imaginatively to enter into the very real poverty in our cities, among aliens, on other continents. We pray not just for them but with them. Because of the nature of Scripture, and of the church, we unwittingly stumble into a solidarity with them. We even discover the profound nature of our own poverty, our shared poverty, with them.

Now back to McCracken. He rotates around the globe, finding melancholy in Washington, England, and Cambodia, and in such historic figures as Konrad Adenauer, Lincoln, and Churchill. Suggesting a way to resist melancholy, and to fulfill the craving of the Psalm, McCracken turns to Luther, who was plagued by dark moods:

"Don't argue with the devil," he said (equating the devil with melancholy). "He has had five thousand years of experience. He has tried out all his tricks on Adam, Abraham and David, and he knows exactly the weak spots. And he is persistent. If he doesn't get you down with the first assault, he will commence a siege of attrition until you give in from sheer exhaustion. Better banish the whole subject. Seek company and discuss some irrelevant matter as, for example, what is going on in Venice. Shun solitude. Eve got into trouble when she walked in the garden alone. I have my worst temptations when I am by myself. Seek convivial company, feminine company, dine, dance, joke and sing. Make yourself eat and drink even though food may be very distasteful. Fasting is the worst expedient." There were ecclesiastics in Luther's day who were shocked by such advice, as there are church people today who cannot bring themselves to credit that he ever offered such advice. Luther, though, went on to strike a deeper note. "Seek out some Christian brother, some wise counselor. Undergird yourself with the fellowship of the church."[24]

While he does not mention it in his sermon, McCracken puts his finger on the solution offered by the Psalm itself—going to be with the company of Zion, as we will see in another sermon on Psalm 42 later in this chapter. Ironically the cure to our own despair may be exactly what is going on in Venice, in not being alone, absorbed in poor me and mine.

Monsters and Wonders

The images we find in the Psalms not only shape but even limit where our imaginations go. The Spanish painter Goya attached a wise remark to his etching, *El sueño de la razon produce monstruous*: "Imagination abandoned by reason produces impossible monsters: united with her, she is the mother of the arts and the source of her wonders."[25] The Psalms invite us to press the limits, and trust us by giving us considerable license to enter into their images. But there must be some reasonable boundaries. Augustine warned us: "However, the truth of valid inference was not instituted by men; rather it was observed by men and set down that they might learn or teach it. For it is perpetually instituted by God in the reasonable order of things."[26]

Sometimes a little common sense would do the preacher much good. Reinhold Niebuhr, in a sermon on Psalm 2:4 ("He that sitteth in the heavens shall laugh" [KJV]), explored in impressive depth the phenomenon of laughter and its relationship to faith. "Humour is a prelude to faith," "The intimate relation between humour and faith is derived from the fact that both deal with the incongruities of our existence," and "Laughter is a vestibule to the Temple of confession"; the victims of tyranny used laughter as a weapon, as it "provided them with a little private world in which they could transvalue the values of the tyrant, and reduce his pompous power to the level of the ridiculous."[27] As psychologically probing and theologically interesting as all this may be, the flaw rests in that the Psalm speaks of the laughter of the one who sits in the heavens, not the laughter of those of us down here on earth. We may wish

Niebuhr had applied his genius to explicate this divine laughter, not our own.

Some attempts at exploring an image are just trivial, too banal to carry the freight of the Gospel. This is a judgment call, of course. But when George Truett preached on Psalm 91:6, "the destruction that wasteth at noonday" became the perils of middle age. Clovis Chappell, popular pastor and evangelist in the southeastern United States, in treating Psalm 107:23-24, explored the image of the mariner, the one who goes down to the sea on a ship. He saw the seafarer as a risk taker, then plunged swiftly to the spiritual risks we take—choosing a livelihood, marrying, having children. To Chappell, our bets should be placed, not surprisingly, upon our faith, upon Jesus Christ, the solid rock. But these are Chappell's thoughts about life, very tenuously attached after the fact to a convenient text. The preacher's bets should be placed on what is in some way really tied in to the sense of the original text, never just grabbing a word and running to familiar turf.

Scholarship may be of great help here. Admittedly the commentaries will reveal that we are not always certain to what each image refers. But knowledge we have gathered over the centuries about the Hebrew text[28] and the biblical world can limit and reshape where the preacher heads. Biblical imagery, utterly commonplace to women and men living in Palestine three thousand years ago, may be strange to ours. "Horn" may for us be a pointed appurtenance on male livestock, but for them the horn was a symbol of strength and dignity. "A flowing stream" may conjure up in our minds the Allegheny or Missouri River, but for them something more shallow, winding, amenable to wading, or even water surprisingly flowing across a sandy bed that most of the year was bone dry. Even the treasured image of a "shepherd": we probably conjure up a pastoral scene with a gentle, well-coiffed man bearing a well-carved staff, handsome and serene; but the first real shepherd one of us saw in Palestine was wearing jeans, yellow boots, and an Elvis T-shirt, swatting and hollering Arabic expletives at his unruly flock.

And so a pilgrimage to the Holy Land could do the preacher some good. Failing that, to immerse yourself in a book of photos, in a dictionary, or even in a travel guide book[29] may spark the imagination and in a more faithful manner; the steep grade of ground rising like bookends around the Jordan; the bone-dry wadis, engulfed by water, but only during the sporadic rainy times; the rich green valleys between Megiddo and Nazareth; the grim, menacing, stony desert zones; the mountain goats defying gravity, birds in flight, fig trees and olive vines, the wilting sun, snow lingering on Mount Hermon.

Dreams and Thanks

Two more examples. In Psalm 126, we hear the Israelites singing, "We are like those who dream." Lest the preacher be tempted to launch into an exploration of our dreams of success, or Martin Luther King, Jr.'s dream of black and white children holding hands, the sobering fact is that in biblical times, the word *dream* described experiences people had while sleeping, never while awake. The "dreaming" in question probably is like the dream of Joseph or the Pharaoh or Mary's Joseph—a nocturnal moment of revelation when God vouchsafes the divine plans for the future. The sermon, therefore, should invite us to be like (not to be, but to be like) Joseph, with a confident glimpse into the future revealed to us by God through Scripture, thereby freed to act boldly and faithfully.

We may also notice how frequently the Psalms speak of giving "thanks." For us, gratitude is a mood, an emotion, almost like good manners. But many times in the Psalter, *thanks* is the English rendering for the Hebrew *todah*, which actually is a tangible sacrifice. Mere words are too cheap, so deep is the Psalmist's gratitude to God. The farmer demonstrates his gratitude by bringing the first ripened stalk of grain as a sacrifice; the shepherd brings his prize male from the herd. So Spurgeon, for all his beautiful words, misses the mark on Psalm 116:17: "Being thy servant, I am bound to sacrifice to thee, and having received spiritual blessings at thy hands I will not bring bullock or goat, but I will bring that which is more suitable, namely, the thanksgiving of my heart. My inmost soul shall adore thee in gratitude."[30]

Our life with God, therefore, may take on a tangibility. If we do not spiritualize sacrifice, we may actually make a sacrifice. Mother Teresa once said, "Giving is not just what you can live without, but what you can't live without, or don't want to live without, something you really like. Then your gift becomes a sacrifice, which will have value before God. Giving until it hurts is what I call love in action."[31] For the preacher is not finally left with pages of images that function like those ink blots the psychotherapist places before his client. The sermon that enters into a metaphor or an image does not proceed finally by random association. Each image, as scriptural, does a different kind of work on a listener. Each image explodes into recognition, dismantling the way we had previously imagined the world to be, surprising us, evoking much that is deep, burrowing out a passageway to a new world. For the Psalter's images are pregnant with hope.

Images of Hope

Just as human distress is beyond words, so it is that comfort, God's presence, also demands a profound metaphor. Psalm 131 bears a startling image of the care and tenderness of God. "I have calmed and quieted my soul like a child quieted at its mother's breast"(RSV). A pilgrim on journey toward the Temple can sing that "even the sparrow finds a home, and the swallow a nest for herself" (Psalm 84:3). God is a fortress, "my rock in whom I take refuge" (Psalm 18:2). "He will cover you with his pinions, and under his wings you will find refuge" (Psalm 91:4). God is light, God is like the rising sun, God's law is more to be desired than "much fine gold; sweeter also than honey" (Psalm 19:10). The one who loves that law is like a tree planted by the river (Psalm 1:3). Unity among brothers is like oil running down a beard, like the dew on Mount Hermon (Psalm 133). Indeed, as Paul Ricoeur has said, "Poetic language alone restores to us that participation-in or belonging-to an order of things which precedes our capacity to oppose ourselves to things taken as objects opposed to a subject."[32]

Some of the Psalter's hopeful images may make modern minds uncomfortable, and stand in need of translation, or some insightful comprehension. Repeatedly God is likened to a fierce warrior, and the preacher must carefully sift through the connotations and ramifications of what this image meant back then and how it is heard today, honoring its ability to reveal something crucial about God. A whole complex of Psalms (47, 93, 96-99) proclaim that the Lord is "king." The negative associations we attach to kingship are many.

Gender, the "maleness" of God, poses challenges preachers solve in various ways. The political nuances rank high as we struggle to fashion a theology around a God who is indeed powerful, but not despotic. Certainly within the Psalter we detect a manner of ruling perhaps at odds with what most earthly potentates have been about—and as Christians we follow Jesus who perfectly embodied what kingship was meant to be, and is with God, and most certainly will be in the fullness of time, however incomprehensible to iron-fisted rulers like Pontius Pilate.

We certainly need some provocation to become at all adept at praise. Trivial subjects are "praised" in advertising, in the arrangements of malls, in our culture's valuations, everything from cars to sneakers, from soap to gadgets. The Psalms are models, trailblazing guides for us who need to rub our eyes and refocus on our destiny, which is to love and praise God (just as Calvin spoke of the Scriptures as spectacles). The Psalms, when preached effectively, will renew our vision, so we might recognize God's love, so we would know why Daniel Hardy and David Ford wrote that praise is "an attempt to cope with the abundance of God's love."[33] The preacher urges his congregation to praise, whether they are ready to praise yet or not; for we begin the practice of praising, and in the midst of it discover we truly do extol and love the God we have been routinely praising. Truly we were created to praise God, and we will never be satisfied until we are "lost in wonder, love, and praise" (Charles Wesley).

Indeed, by the workings of God's grace, the ability of an image, a mere word, to bear grace and hope grows over time. Many images carry the freight of the faith of our parents or grandparents, the weight of past moments of healing or deliverance. To sing "Amazing Grace"—"was blind, but now I see"—taps not only into some reservoir of hopeful memory in our souls but also into a great tradition of family members, and saints of old, who prayed and sang the Psalms and continue to do so. Hardy and Ford eloquently suggest that "traditional language can give cups for meaning which are gradually filled up over the years as experience and knowledge grow and the key words and concepts (such as glory, salvation, holy, grace, cross, resurrection, Lord, wisdom, Spirit, love, confession, peace and many others) grow in content."[34]

The Psalter, charged as it is with the realities of our world and its cries for justice, offers hope to peoples and nations. To name injustice, to cry out to God and in God's name, is the first and necessary step out of inertia, toward change, an end to apathy. Augustine's famous saying is pertinent here: "Hope has two beautiful daughters, anger and courage. Anger at the way things are, courage to see to it they do not remain as they are."[35]

While the exploration of an image or metaphor may provide the preacher with an entrée to a Psalm, other approaches may help. A given image is like a still life, as the eye zooms in on that particular portrait. Time comes to a halt as we examine it. But there is also movement within each Psalm. A throng of worshipers bustle down a dusty road. Trumpets are lifted, hands clap. Moods swing abruptly. The preacher needs to keep pace with the movement within the Psalm, to sense where it is going, and to make that journey with the congregation. The following sermon on Psalm 42 begins by stopping to explore an image, a deer sniffing the air for water, with a counter image of another creature surrounded by water, but no less desperate. But then the sermon stirs into motion with the Psalmist, following his movement, which is at once geographical but also psychological and even theological.

Psalm 42: The Beauty and Urgency of My Song

"As a deer longs for flowing streams, so my soul longs for you, O God."[36] This Psalmist had seen a deer, probably many of them, thirsty, nosing about, peering into dry riverbeds, searching for water—and he knew that he thirsted for God in the same way. You can create your own image for this quest. In Pat Conroy's novel, *The Lords of Discipline,* young Will McLean laments his lack of a romantic life in words that may reflect our anxiety about God:

> I once read in a book that traced the natural history of blue whales that the great creatures often had to travel thousands of miles through the dark waters of the Pacific to find a mate. They conducted their search with the fever and furious attention of beasts aware of the imminence of extinction. As whaling fleets depleted their numbers, scientists conjectured that there were whales who would exhaust themselves in fruitless wandering and never connect with any mate at all. When I read about those solitary

leviathans, I feared I had stumbled on an allegory of my own life, that I would spend my life unable to make a connection, unable to find someone attracted by the beauty and urgency of my song.[37]

There's a psychology to this thirst. Our seeking, our song, is indeed urgent—but it has a beauty about it. You don't need me to tell you that we walk around with this gaping hole in our souls, and we will pour anything and everything into it to fill it: stuff, diversions, booze, you name it. We view this thirst as a problem—one to be solved, and quickly. But maybe that hole isn't a curse so much as a gift. That hollowness is God crying out to you; your song is God's song first! God's Spirit has burrowed out a place so you would seek after him. Otherwise, you might never sense any need for God. It gets mislabeled—but it is God's call. And the answer isn't something far away. Augustine said, "The divine mystery is closer to me than I am to myself." And he also said, "O Lord, you have made us for yourself, and our hearts are restless until they find rest in you."[38]

It may be we miss out on this because of the economics of the Psalm. We are utterly unacquainted with thirst. At the Howell house, we have water in multiple locations, in six rooms, and in several spigots outside. We also have bottles of Midas Spring Water, superior water, there for our choosing. We know nothing of what the ancients knew all too well: what it was like to fall on your knees, look upward to the heavens, and know that the gathering clouds and what God might shower on the earth were matters of life and death, not just bad news for an impending picnic. Water, even for us, is no luxury, but a necessity. It permeates all that we are. But as affluent as we are, we take all that for granted; and it is hard to glimpse our dependence upon God. To figure it out, we need to go to school, we need some discipline.

There is an aspect of time and effort to this Psalm. The Psalmist prays this prayer in the far north of Israel, at the foot of snow-capped Mount Hermon, where even today there is a spectacular waterfall that forms the source of the Jordan River. He prays there, but he longs to go up to Jerusalem—and that will take some time, some labor, a lot of energy, a plan. There is a time lapse, and the need for some exerted effort, between when he prays and when the fulfillment might come.

Prayer, connecting with God, is never quick and easy. It's like learning a foreign language. Fifteen years ago I studied Italian in some depth. Then I flew to Italy, thinking I'd be proficient. But prowling around Rome, I soon was lost, getting just bits and pieces here and there. But I kept at it, immersed myself in my confusion, took even embarrassing stabs at it—and finally, in about the fourth week, something clicked. A real conversation, back and forth, in Italian. I even began to have some Italian thoughts!

Now it's no use trying Italian on me on your way out of church today—because I have spoken and listened to virtually no Italian since then. I am having no Italian thoughts at all. Prayer is like that, like a muscle. It requires use, discipline. All the great masters of prayer teach us this. Dom John Chapman said, "The only way to pray is to pray; the only way to pray well is to pray much."[39] Catherine of Siena wrote, "You, O God, are a deep sea into which, the more I enter, the more I find, and the more I find, the more I seek."[40] Joseph Cardinal Bernadin, while dying of cancer, gave us, who suddenly fire off those 911 prayers when we are in trouble, this shrewd advice: "Pray while you're well, because when you're sick you will not feel well enough to pray."[41] And Georges Bernanos said we must block out a time for prayer each day: even if not well used, don't give it to anybody else!

This leads us to the geography of Psalm 42. The Psalmist knows that God is everywhere; he is praying, after all, near Mount Hermon. But there is a place, somewhere he needs to go. Henry David Thoreau went into the woods "because I wished to live deliberately, to front only the essential facts of life, and see if I could not learn what it had to teach, and not, when I came to die, discover that I had not lived."[42] The Israelites came out of the woods and went to the Temple on Mount Zion, God's holy city. When they thought of that Temple, they subscribed to what Amos Wilder once said about church: "Going to church is like approaching an open volcano, where the world is molten and hearts are sifted. The altar is like a rail that spatters sparks, the sanctuary like the chamber next to an atomic oven. There are invisible rays, and you leave your watch outside."[43]

They knew God certainly was everywhere, but they were aware of it because of what happened in the Temple, in those special meetings in public worship. Nowadays, attendance at worship is regarded as utterly optional; in fact, some feel you can probably be a better Christian if you don't go and suffer the distractions and hypocrisy and parking stress. Church is treated as a matter of convenience, something you do on Sunday if there's not too much else going on. And you might even enjoy it, if the choir sings pretty, if the preacher is funny.

But we are wired by God in such a way that we need to be in worship. We owe it to God. And we need the pace and the impact of the words uttered only there. As T. S. Eliot wrote, "Why should men love the Church? . . . She tells them of evil and sin, and other unpleasant facts."[44]

Today we celebrate Holy Communion. The Psalmist poignantly remarks that tears have been my bread day and night. Have tears, sorrow, been your bread? At the Temple there was another bread, called the bread of presence, just a loaf of bread that somehow signified to the Jews the very face of God. I wonder if Jesus had that in mind at the Last Supper when he took a loaf of bread, blessed it, broke it, and gave it to them saying "This is my body, given for you." It was Jesus who said I am the living water, and I am the bread of life. The bread I give for the life of the world is my body. And on the cross, when Jesus flung open a window into the very heart of God to show us his mercy, his side was pierced and out flowed water—a sign, a symbol, that this Jesus whom we worship in this place, around this table, is what we are thirsty for.

Flannery O'Connor was once asked what really mattered in her life. She said that it was this bread: "Holy Communion is the center of existence for me. All the rest is expendable." And so it is. As a deer longs for flowing streams, so my soul longs for you, O God. When shall I come and behold the face of God? God is here. Now. Today. Your beautiful song has been heard.

CHAPTER 5

The Dynamics of Movement

While the images in the Psalms may function like still-life paintings, and a sermon might capture that luminescence, the Psalms do not sit still on the page, but witness to bustling activity, in this and that direction, people trekking across the countryside and about Mount Zion, physically moving toward God and toward each other. So a second approach to preaching a Psalm may be to capture its inner dynamic, the energy that transports the reader to a new place. We enter the Psalm at a particular point, in some situation, with a certain mood. But the Psalm leaves us at a surprising destination, in a new situation with an altered mood. We may construe this movement in various ways, depending on the Psalm. In the case of Psalm 42 we simply notice the Psalmist making a swift mental pilgrimage south to Jerusalem, which if traversed on foot would not be just another trip, but would be fraught with personal transformation.

Let us think about how this movement happens in the Psalms. Logically the most primal movement began in the hazy recesses of time when some synapse fired in someone's head, when the ground was parched—or perhaps after the rain finally fell, and that *homo sapiens* raised his or her eyes very high and cried out for help or gave thanks for the help. This basic move of transcendence developed and was articulated in the Psalms in fascinating ways. We know much about the gestures used in prayer, about the organized liturgical life that was exuberant, and the preacher needs to be familiar with the manner of private and public prayer through commentaries and other studies.[1] Hands were stretched upward. The body was prostrated on the ground. Dancers did somersaults. Trumpets blared. Smoke curled heavenward. Services were timed so the light broke through a Temple aperture at the right moment.

The *Sitz im Leben*

We may need some sense of archaeology and geography, of psychology and sociology. Perhaps the place to begin is to notice how scholars have taken a Psalm and surmised its *Sitz im Leben*, its probable "setting in life." Hermann Gunkel, at the turn into the twentieth century, convinced most of the thinking world that the Psalms were not just pious lyrics, but originated in the normal round of worship, at the great festivals, at the coronation of the king, prior to the army departing for battle, during pilgrimages.

Clever scholars have devised complex liturgical scenarios that could have undergirded the Psalms we now hear. Sigmund Mowinckel suggested that the "enthronement Psalms" (47, 93, 96-99) were sung at an annual festival, at New Year's, celebrating the enthronement of Israel's God, Yahweh. Hans-Joachim Kraus focused on the "royal Psalms" (45, 72, 110) and proposed an annual Royal Zion Festival, celebrating God's unique presence on Mount Zion and his election of David and his descendants to be kings. Artur Weiser imagined the Psalms punctuating a Covenant Renewal Festival. None of these has corralled a consensus of opinion from scholars. We just cannot peek behind the Psalter and document festivals never actually mentioned in the Bible. But the impulse of Mowinckel, Kraus, and Weiser is not mistaken. Beyond any question, although we are ignorant of the details and timing, the Psalms surely emerged out of a fascinating, vibrant life of worship. As such, the Psalms give evidence of a vigorous, enthusiastic kind of worship, pulsating with sound and motion, titillating us with visuals and scents.

Great caravans would traverse rocky roads, the pilgrims singing Psalm 84, "My soul longs, yea, faints for the courts of the LORD" (RSV). Their destination? Jerusalem—and much of what transpires in the Psalms is located in Jerusalem. The preacher may hold the ancient city well in mind, how it was fixed on a narrow spur spreading northward, looming above the Kidron Valley across from the Mount of Olives.[2] The preacher may wish to portray its massive stone walls, punctuated by gates and towers. Whole Psalms are devoted to the glory of the city of God (Psalms 48, 76), which itself stands as an image of God.

The focal point was the Temple. Solomon's sanctuary was splendid, and after the exile it was rebuilt on a slightly less grand scale; while not as opulent, the Temple was still the heart of Israel's world, a window to paradise. The symbolism of the Temple is reflected in many Psalms: the panels and stonework of the Temple were decorated with trees, flowers, fruit. But we should not imagine the Temple as a still life! Its precincts were a swirl of activity. Widen your gaze and look at the throng of pilgrims, who have braved the elements in their caravans, crowding around the hill of Mount Zion. The shofar blares, smoke curls heavenward, and as the ark of the covenant is hoisted aloft at the head of a processional into the Temple precincts, the people cry out in deafening unison:

> The LORD, the Most High, is awesome,
>   a great king over all the earth. (Psalm 47:2)

Their worship is enthusiastic, with dancing, lyre, harp, pipes, trumpet, drums, cymbals. Their music was inspired by God, and certainly an offering to God, yet surely revelatory of God. Worship was downright noisy:

> Clap your hands, all peoples!
> Shout to God with loud songs of joy! . . .
>
> God has gone up with a shout,
>   the LORD with the sound of a trumpet.
> Sing praises to God, sing praises! (Psalm 47:1, 5 RSV)

And then there is that even more deafening moment of stillness:

> Be still, and know that I am God! (Psalm 46:10)

Dare you smell the burning fat and oozing blood of lambs, burnt on the altar, while words of faith are sung:

> I will offer to thee burnt offerings of fatlings,
>   with the smoke of the sacrifice of rams; . . .

Come and hear, all you who fear God,
    and I will tell what he has done for me. (Psalm 66:15, 16)

Movement, Not Principles

Apart from ancient people surging up the hill of Zion, there is a verbal, personal kind of movement within each Psalm. We should always be cautious of zeroing in too closely on some small piece of a Psalm without attending to the dynamics of the whole. The preacher must avoid a tempting detour illustrated too often in the history of preaching the Psalms. Martin Lloyd-Jones preached a long series of sermons on Psalm 73 while minister of Westminster Chapel, London.[3] The sheer number of sermons, proceeding portion by portion, insures that the flow of the Psalm will be lost in the verbiage. But Lloyd-Jones's approach to each section is alien to the nature of the Psalter. He reads a verse or two, and then asks, "What are the lessons to be learned here?" He speaks of "deductions," and finds "certain principles" in the Psalm. This kind of sheer rationality is dangerous, and shields the listener from being drawn into the organic vitality of a dynamic Psalm that is most definitely going someplace.

Preachers have always searched for subtle shifts in the Psalms. Rufus Jones, the great Quaker who died in 1948, tried to capture the internal movement of the Twenty-third Psalm. The Psalm "begins with innocence," just as life does. The second stage of life is harder, not so instinctual, but a struggle, hard work. Finally there is a third stage of life, when we have achieved a wisdom enabling us toward a "secondary instinct," wherein we have learned a skill so thoroughly it is like an instinct. We knit without watching our hands.

Expounding the first verse of the first Psalm, Spurgeon noted its trio of verbs characterizing the ungodly: *walk, stand, sit.*

> When men are living in sin they go from bad to worse. At first they merely *walk* in the counsel of the careless and *ungodly*, who forget God—the evil is rather practical than habitual—but after that, they become habituated to evil, and they *stand* in the way of open *sinners* who willfully violate God's commandments; and if let alone, they go one step further, and become themselves pestilent teachers and tempters of others, and thus they *sit in the seat of*

the scornful. They have taken their degree in vice, and as true Doctors of Damnation they are installed.[4]

Whether the preacher wishes to make so much of the sequence, Spurgeon does call attention to something in the text not usually noticed.

When expostulating on Psalm 6, Spurgeon notes a shift around verse 8: "The Psalmist has changed his note. He leaves the minor key, and betakes himself to sublime strains. He tunes his note in the high key of confidence."[5] The most basic movement is from lament to praise. In dozens of Psalms we hear a cry for help, so basic to being human in a world where the "center does not hold," and where people dare to look upward for help. But there is in virtually every lament an inevitable, surprising turn to hopeful praise.

From Lament to Praise

The laments emerged in situations where an individual was sorely troubled and came to the sanctuary to plead for clemency, to cry out for divine aid. Joachim Begrich penned an article ("Das priesterliche Heilsorakel") in 1934 that explained the sudden shift in mood and perspective, this movement to praise. Begrich suggested that an "oracle of salvation" would be uttered by a priest in the midst of the Psalmist's prayer, and even in the regular usage of such prayers. We see examples of this in the narrative books: Hannah is pouring out her agony at Shiloh, and the old priest, Eli, after discerning that she is not in fact drunk, speaks a blessing: "Go in peace, and the God of Israel grant your petition" (1 Samuel 1:17 RSV). Hezekiah, perilously ill, prays for healing (2 Kings 20:2), and the prophet Isaiah articulates God's answer: "Thus says the Lord, . . . I have heard your prayer, I have seen your tears; behold, I will heal you" (vv. 5-6 RSV).

The Psalms take up this abrupt turn, typically with the hopeful word *but.* Psalm 13 cries, "How long, O LORD? . . . Consider and answer me!" Then the turn: "But I have trusted in thy steadfast love; / my heart shall rejoice in thy salvation" (v. 5 RSV). Not only individuals, but the gathered worshiping community expected some word, a response from God, voiced by the priest. In Psalm 85, the community cries out for help: "Show us your steadfast love, O

LORD, and grant us your salvation." Immediately a voice chimes in with: "Let me hear what God the LORD will speak, / for he will speak peace to his people." This transition is the ultimate witness to the reality of God, to the good news of God's activity in human life.

What this means, and those who have never heard of Begrich can sense it, is that the Psalms are dialogical. Few Psalms are monologues; most capture both sides of a conversation. Hurt, anxiety, and confession are articulated—but there is an answer, the answer of faith, the surprise of God's graciousness, the ray of hope. The sermon must carry out both sides of this conversation as well, as the preacher voices our pain but also the answer, the opening of a window to healing.

From what we know of the laments, this healing happens two ways. First, the very fact of naming the chaos and confusion in our lives and world is a first and necessary step in healing. When the preacher rivets our attention to the cry "Wake up, arouse yourself, O Lord! How long?" we immediately feel more at home than we did a moment before. We are no longer isolated. The word gives form and shape to our flailing in the morass; and once it has some shape, we can objectify it, examine it, and hold it securely enough to lift it upward toward God.[6]

This primal task requires a probing diagnosis of the human condition that is unabashedly theological. We do not assume that a worshiper understands the hollowness he feels, the craziness of her life. In fact, it is only in the light of the Gospel that we come to a true comprehension of what is out of sync, of where the dysfunction truly lies. To name the malady is risky, and daring, assuming an authority a listener may not at first grant. In our culture, as Wade Clark Roof has noted, people "are inclined to regard their own experiences as superior to the accounts of others, and the truths found through self-discovery as having greater relevance to them than those handed down by way of creed or custom."[7]

The preacher's challenge therefore is to be as persuasive and truthful as possible, hoping that some recognition kicks in as we portray the plight and hope of humanity. This portrayal requires sensitivity and even a humility. The preacher may in his heart believe that "the problem" is simply sin; the reason we feel the waters have come up to our neck, the reason for our bleak hopelessness, is that we suffer disbelief, that we have erected barriers between our lives and the giver of life, and our misdeeds are finding us out. Whether this diagnosis is accurate or not may not matter if we fail to put our finger on the reality perched in the pew before us. The confession, "We have sinned against thy holy laws," may be utter nonsense to people, simply because they don't even know what God's holy laws are in the first place. Douglas John Hall has explained why modern North Americans are not so much like Prometheus, defiantly scaling the heights and stealing what properly is God's; rather we are like Sisyphus, seemingly condemned to struggle to push some massive stone up a hill, only to have it tumble down once we get close to the top.[8] Sinners we may be; but first and foremost, we are exhausted, and don't even know why. Nowhere is our utter weariness better understood than in the Psalter. "How long, O Lord?"

The Rain Is Over

But the Psalm does not merely make the human predicament palpable. The stunning movement within virtually every Psalm of lament from plea to praise, from cry to trust, bears witness not merely to the faith of some poet three millennia gone by. That drama of lament moving to praise is an effective, powerful word for those who dare to pray the Psalm—and the preacher must capture that same transformation of mood. Let us hear Spurgeon once more, on the turn from lament to praise just after Psalm 13:4.

> What a change is here! Lo, the rain is over and gone, and the time of the singing of birds is come. The mercy-seat has so refreshed the poor weeper, that he clears his throat for a song. If we have mourned with him, let us now dance with him. David's heart was more often out of tune than his harp. He begins many of his Psalms sighing, and ends them singing.

Then he captures something essential: "It is worthy to be observed that the joy is all the greater because of the previous sorrow."[9] Credit for this shift, in Spurgeon's view, is divine: "The Holy Spirit had wrought into the Psalmist's mind the confidence that his prayer was heard."[10]

Brueggemann, following Paul Ricoeur, has devised helpful labels: from our well-ordered, stable world, expressed in hymns of praise, the lament Psalms are disorienting, probing into our situations of dislocation; but the movement is always to reorientation.[11] And this reorientation is surely more profound than an untested, naïve faith. This is the meaning of disillusionment: Our illusions are swept away.[12] We discover that our simplistic mental arrangements about God are inadequate to cope with the realities of life. The sermon strives to guide people through a maze of anguish to arrive at what Ricoeur called a "second naïveté," a trust that is sober and mature, sculpted out of hard experience. Hardy and Ford, considering human shame, and its healing via the shame of the cross of Christ, argue that "shame can only be overcome by something that takes its distorted non-order seriously and meets it with a more powerful genuine non-order."[13]

Two warnings, though. The preacher fails if a sermon on a lament is trivialized into sunny optimism. The distinction between optimism and hope has become well known. Martin Luther King, Jr., not long before his assassination, shared with his old Dexter Avenue Baptist Church that although he still had hope, he was no longer optimistic. Optimism depends on us getting our acts together, on "things" working out comfortably; but hope depends on God. The thought is nowhere better described than by Christopher Lasch:

> Hope does not demand a belief in progress. It demands a belief in justice: a conviction that the wicked will suffer, that wrongs will be made right, that the underlying order of things is not flouted with impunity. Hope implies a deep-seated trust in life that appears absurd to those who lack it. It rests on confidence not so much in the future as in the past. . . . If we distinguish hopefulness from the more conventional attitude known today as optimism, . . . we can see why it serves us better, in steering troubled waters ahead, than a belief in progress. Not that it prevents us from expecting the worst. The worst is always what the hopeful are prepared for. Their trust in life would not be worth much if it had not survived disappointments in the past, while the knowledge that the future holds further disappointments demonstrates the continuing need for hope.[14]

He concludes this incisive section, saying that "a blind faith that things will somehow work out for the best, furnishes a poor substitute for the disposition to see things through even when they don't." No pithy advice allowed here: A sermon that is faithful to the Psalter will never say, "Time heals" or "Things work out" or any merely natural outcome of difficulty. The Psalmists knew a God who intervened, who brought light out of darkness, a God for whom nothing is ever impossible.

A second caveat: Our tendency may be to hurry prematurely to the Psalm's end, to short-circuit our groveling and wallowing in the mire. Worshipers are told far too often to have faith, to trust God, to be hopeful—the advice all good, but it all papers over the need the faithful have to cry out, to look darkness in the eye, to understand and let out into the open our wounds and craziness. To explore the mire at some length is not faithless! If the Psalms teach us anything, it is that we have license to hurt, to doubt, to scream in agony, as did the Psalmists, as did Job, as did Jeremiah, as did Jesus himself, who did not hurry to a serene faith on the cross, but drew upon a Psalm to voice the worst dereliction imaginable.

Public Prayer

The Psalter also embodies a movement that is relentlessly corporate, drawing us out of our isolation, reminding us of our public relationships. Many Psalms are community laments. Perhaps on great fast days, the Israelites would gather for prayer and sacrifice, their concerns being public and international in flavor (see Jeremiah 36, Psalms 44, 74). Although their need to do so is tremendous, not many congregations will resonate easily to community laments. Brueggemann is right:

> So while the personal laments may parallel experiences of our own, the loss of public experience means we have little experiential counterpart to the communal laments. Given our privatistic inclination, we do not often think about public disasters as concerns for prayer life. If we do, we treat them as somehow a lesser item. We have nearly lost our capacity to think *theologically* about public issues and public problems. Even more, we have lost our capacity to practice prayer in relationship to public events.[15]

To explore public events prayerfully, the preacher needs to be apprenticed at the feet of the heroes of the pulpit for whom this capacity was second nature. John Chrysostom brought the Psalms and all of Scripture to bear on public and social issues in Antioch and then Constantinople, setting off riots and getting himself banished from the empire. Sojourner Truth, Martin Luther King, Jr., Oscar Romero, Desmond Tutu—all can stand as models to train the preacher in defying the persistent privatism of the church, and of our own souls.[16]

From Loneliness to Community

Even when we think of the individual laments, there is a community aspect to these prayers. The movement from lament to praise parallels a movement from isolation to community. We see this parallel most clearly in the Psalms of thanksgiving (such as Psalms 30, 66), which dramatically unveil what can transpire in the days and weeks after the lament is voiced. God has rescued the individual, who had felt crushed and hopeless, who bargained boldly with God pleading for aid. In the thanksgiving, the one who has been saved brings a sacrifice of thanks, but does so in the company of family, friends, the worshiping community. With the sacrifice still crackling on the altar, the one delivered speaks to God ("I thank you"), then turns and speaks to those present, and bears witness to what God has done. No more powerful expression of the Good News could be imagined than the personal testimony of one who "once was lost, but now am found." The preacher needs to capture and even retell such stories of deliverance—but with an eye to this crucial movement from loneliness to belonging. For if the original plea for help was uttered in isolation, then the thanksgiving illustrates how the lonely lamenter has been restored to the life of the community and for that moment stands at its center as its latest witness to not only his own fellowship with God but that of the community as well.

The very act in worship of uniting voices in song creates community in a peculiar way, noted by David Ford:

> Sounds do not have exclusive boundaries—they can blend, harmonise, resonate with each other in endless ways. In singing there can be a filling of space with sound in ways that draw more

and more voices to take part, yet with no sense of crowding. It is a performance of abundance, as new voices join in with their own distinctive tones. There is an "edgeless expansion" (Begbie), an overflow of music, in which participants have their boundaries transformed. The music is both outside and within them, and it creates a new vocal, social space of community in song. . . . There is no end to its enrichment, and it enables one to imagine how each singer can be valued and have something distinctive to offer while yet being given to the complex unity of the singing.[17]

This unity into which the Psalmist was drawn, and into which we who worship today are drawn, extends over place and time as well. Let us listen to Ford once again:

So the Psalmist's "I" accommodates a vast congregation of individuals and groups down the centuries and around the world today. They are all somehow embraced in this "I." A vast array of stories, situations, sufferings, blessings, joys and deaths have been read and prayed into the Psalms by those who have identified with their first person. It amounts to an extraordinarily capacious and hospitable "I."[18]

Movement Within the Psalter

Diodore of Tarsus, noticing for instance that Psalm 3 is dated to David's crisis with Absalom, while Psalm 143 is dated to his battle with Goliath, argues that the order of the Psalms is random. And why? "Because the book was lost during the captivity in Babylon, and was found afterwards, during the time of Ezra—not the whole book together, but scattered in groups of one, two, or perhaps three Psalms. And they were put together just as they were found, not as they had been composed in the beginning."[19] Is there anything to be made out of the placement of a Psalm alongside its neighbors? Perhaps. Introducing Psalm 23, Spurgeon suggested,

The position of this Psalm is worthy of notice. It follows the twenty-second, which is peculiarly the Psalm of the Cross. There are no green pastures, no still waters on the other side of the twenty-second Psalm. It is only after we have read, "My God, my God, why hast thou forsaken me!" that we come to "The Lord is my Shepherd." We must by experience know the value of blood-shedding, and see the sword awakened against the Shepherd, before we shall be able to know the sweetness of the good Shepherd's care.[20]

Gerald Wilson has argued that the Psalter as a whole seems to be shaped with this movement from lament to praise in mind. The darker Psalms of lament, those desperate pleas for help, are concentrated in the first half of the book, the second half leaning clearly toward notes of praise.[21] Brueggemann has gone further, discerning the way Psalm 1 begins the book with the theme of obedience, while Psalm 150 concludes the book with a paean of praise. He argues that obedience to God pushes us toward praising God; but that praise itself is virtually the transcendence of obedience, as we discover joyous communion as the ultimate good toward which the obedient, faithful life points. How he can surmise the intent of the editors of the Psalter is unclear. But structurally he is certainly correct to notice that "to move from Psalm 1 at the beginning to Psalm 150 at the end, one must depart from the *safe world* of Psalm 1 and plunge into the middle of the Psalter where one will find a world of *enraged suffering*. In its laments, Israel protests against the simplistic theological affirmations of Psalm 1."[22]

In a sense, the entire Old Testament, and by extension the entire Bible, bears witness to this movement from lament to praise, from distress to deliverance. The Bible is filled with such cries of lamentation, from the lips of Abraham, Hagar, Rebecca, Hannah, Job, Jeremiah, Paul, Jesus. In Exodus, the Israelites groan under the Pharaoh's fist; God answers dramatically, and the people sing and dance the sheer delight only freed people understand. Hungry, they cry out for bread; and manna rains down on them. Harassed by Philistines and Midianites, they plead for aid; and God raises up Gideon and Samson. Elijah prays for a dead child, who is revived. Hemmed in by Sennacherib, Hezekiah rends his garments in supplication; and the Assyrians are routed. Lamentations poignantly sighs, "There is no one to comfort"; then like a strong tenor, God's prophet pierces the silence: "Comfort, comfort ye my people!" Jesus is moved to compassion by the cries of the centurion, the Gerasene demoniac, blind Bartimaeus, a sinking Peter. His cross and resurrection are in truth the answer to every cry ever raised, from the first *homo sapiens* to children yet to be conceived.

As a sample of the movement from lament to praise, and from Old Testament to New Testament, we share a sermon on Psalm 73, whose themes will be reiterated in chapter 7 in some depth.

Tested by its Own Defeat: A Sermon on Psalm 73

Surely God is good to the pure in heart. I mean, if we developed a job description for God, that should hover near the top. It is God's job to bless, to protect, to do good, and especially for those who are good.[23]

The Psalmist knows this saying, *God is good to the pure in heart,* quite well—but has also learned from the school of his own life that there is this anomaly at the epicenter of life. *But as for me, all the day long I have been stricken.* He has kept his heart pure, he has done the right thing, he has been faithful and good—but has been rewarded with nothing but suffering, physical pain, actual poverty. The number one theological question that lands in my office is his: If there is a good God, then why do people, and especially good people, suffer? Isn't God supposed to bless and protect us?

Why is there suffering? C. S. Lewis, early in his career, traveled around England lecturing on the problem of evil. He said, "Sufferings are God's hammerblows to awaken and to discipline us." But then he got married, and his wife, Joy, suffered the brutality of cancer and died. Lewis never again said, "Sufferings are God's hammerblows." He recognized the painful illogic of his words. God does not give cancer or strike people with AIDS or cause car accidents.

This view that the good are rewarded and the wicked are punished is absurd to anyone with eyes and ears. At my latest check, the rich and healthy are not especially holy. If so, you could just find the largest houses in a city, peer in the windows, and there you would find moral exemplars, saints, champions of good. You could check the obituaries each day; and the people with the high numbers next to their names you could assume to be very righteous, while any who died young must have been guilty of great sin. On that model, if God is "blessing" anybody in America, it must be Bill Gates. But it was Gates who said he didn't understand why people would go to church; it seemed to him like an inefficient use of time. Better to be out working and making money.

The Psalmist tells the truth about our view of at least some of the wealthy—even though we know better. "Pride is their necklace; . . . their hearts overflow with follies . . . their tongue struts through the earth"; but "people turn and praise them,/ and find no fault in them" (RSV). We all know and love somebody who is wealthy, and we want to leap to their defense. But when someone is good, like this Psalmist, but suffers, there is almost a resentment toward those who have plenty and great ease. And there is an implicit warning that attaches itself to wealth, beautifully put by G. K. Chesterton: "There is one thing Christ and all the Christian saints have said with a sort of savage monotony: they have said simply that to be rich is to be in peculiar danger of moral wreck."[24]

We can explain much suffering, without blaming God. When there is an airplane crash, people always ask, "How could God allow this tragedy?" But God doesn't swat planes out of the air. Rather, when Orville and Wilbur Wright lifted off at Kitty Hawk and people watched and said, "Now that's a great way to get around"; we signed a contract with death, knowing fully well that some hopefully small percentage of planes would malfunction and crash. Lots of suffering is like that—and I want to say to those who suffer, "Don't take it personally!"

But nothing could be more personal. The "problem of evil" is no intellectual head game, something intellectuals bat about in some ivory tower. Suffering is intensely personal. It strikes, like a fist to your midsection. It just deflates you. Teddy Roosevelt suffered the death of his wife, Alice, as she was giving birth, and his mother, Mittie, on the same day. At the end of that day, he wrote in his diary: "She was beautiful. . . . when her life seemed just to be begun . . . when my heart's dearest died, the light went out of my life forever."[25]

When we suffer, there is a temptation to give up on God—and many have. I cannot blame them. One of my early hospital visits years ago was with a young woman, in her twenties, whose doctor had just informed her that she would not survive. Late that night, her mother just kept staring out the hospital window into the darkness. When I had to leave, I said, "Can I say a prayer?" She did not turn around and dismissed the thought by saying, "Pray if you want. No one is listening."

I do not blame her. The Psalmist stood with her when he said, *All in vain have I kept my heart clean.* But he doesn't give up. His faith survives somehow, and he gives two reasons for this surprise.

But then I went to the sanctuary of God. He went to the Temple, the holy place; and somehow, by being in that place, he caught some glimpse of hope. I wonder any more what people think about church buildings. Once upon a time in America, the skylines of great cities featured towering church spires. Now they are dwarfed by towers that celebrate commerce, money. In our anti-institutional milieu, many people feel they can virtually be more spiritual outside the church. Many are cynical about church—and I might add, we have labored long and hard to earn that cynicism! But despite whatever may or may not go on inside a church, the very fact that they still stand is awesome. In Lorraine Hansberry's play, *Raisin in the Sun*, a suddenly grown-up girl announces to her mother that she no longer believes in God. Her mother makes a swift path across the room, slaps her daughter on the cheek, and commands, "Repeat after me: In my mother's house, there still is a God." A sanctuary is a protest, a dissenting voice in our culture of skepticism, that there still is a God. They are, admittedly, mere stone. But Jesus once said that even the stones would cry out.

But another reason the Psalmist doesn't give up is implied in verse 15. He speaks of being *untrue to the generation of thy children* (RSV). He is not alone as a believer, a seeker, a doubter; but he is woven into the fabric of a community, of a broader congregation, who have believed. Many have endured much worse and doggedly hung on. I love to read the lives of saints and the stories of martyrs, how they clung to God in the face of vicious attacks and long nights of suffering.

In 1985 I went to China with a colleague who was born there, the child of missionaries. They were driven from the country in 1948—all except his father, and we went in part looking for news of what had happened to him. After poking around, we found a longtime friend, aide, assistant of his father, who told us how his father had languished in jail for some months, had been treated brutally, and had died. He proceeded to tell of his own incarceration, for a couple of decades, treated harshly, his only crime having been his faith in Christ. But as he spoke, there was a peace, a strange joy, a buoyant faith—and I promised myself in that moment that I could never, ever, give up on my faith in Christ—because of this man.

Now, the Psalmist isn't miraculously healed of his diseases. His flesh and heart are still failing. He doesn't win the lottery; Ed McMahon doesn't show up with $10 million. He is still poor; he still suffers. But he affirms now, with great certainty, *Surely God is good to the pure in heart.* He believes it now; he understands it now. But he has redefined each term in the equation.

God is no longer the great cashier in the sky, who rings up your good deeds and with a big "thank you" hands you some payout. No, *God* is the one whose love never fails, the one who is there, who is not trivialized by human schemes of deserving. For Christians, that God has a face, and the contours of that face are the compassion and wisdom and tenderness of Jesus.

And God is *good*. But the *good* that God gives is no "thing." What God gives isn't this or that—but God gives himself. I have things that belonged to my grandfather, Papa Howell: his pocket watch, his mail pouch, his Bible, some tools—and I treasure them above most earthly possessions. But I would eagerly throw them all away to have just one more hour with him, the man himself, talking, laughing, sitting under his oak tree. *For me, it is good to be near God.* Legend has it that when St. Thomas Aquinas, one of the most prolific and profound theologians the church has ever known, was on his deathbed, a voice was heard from somewhere above: "Thomas, you have written well of me. What reward would you ask for yourself?" And Thomas replied, "Nothing but yourself, O Lord." That was the gist of the last of Charles Wesley's hymns, composed on his own deathbed:

> In age and feebleness extreme,
> What shall a sinful worm redeem?
> Jesus, my only hope thou art,
> Strength of my failing flesh and heart;
> O, could I catch a smile from thee,
> And drop into eternity![26]

In the sanctuary a woman in a robe presses a fragment of bread into my palm. I taste the heady wine. *It is good to be near God.* Jesus, the wounded one, is the sanctuary, the benefit, the surprise. And I turn my head and see them all, *the generation of thy children,* surging forward, singing, laughing.

Yes, God is good to the *pure in heart.* And purity of heart is no longer just doing nice things or avoiding grimy things. What comes out of the heart is—love. The pure of heart love. That's what eternal life is about: It's not that we die, and then God gives us this ultimate prize. Rather, we develop a relationship of love with God now that is so strong that even death itself cannot sever it. Sorrow is always mingled with love—but that is our glory. In Rian Malan's great book about South Africa, *My Traitor's Heart,* the most compelling character is named Creina Alcock. She has suffered much. But late in life, she says this:

> Love is worth nothing until it has been tested by its own defeat. Love, even if it ends in defeat, gives you a kind of honor; without love, you have no honor at all. Love enables you to transcend defeat. Love is the only thing that leaves light inside you, instead of the total, obliterating darkness.[27]

We look into the darkness, and it seems no one is listening. Defeat seems too great a test. But there is a candle, flickering in some dark sanctuary, and it dispels the darkness. Through a window we see, we are touched, and we know that *it is good to be near God.* And then it dawns: *Surely God is good to the pure in heart.* And it is enough.

PART III

Preaching the Psalms: What?

CHAPTER 6

The Pursuit of Happiness

In this final section of the book, we turn to look at several theological issues that are essential to consider in some depth for one who would preach the Psalms.[1] We will not even try to offer any complete or systematic "Theology of the Psalms." Such books exist. Attention is often paid to Hans-Joachim Kraus's magisterial *Theology of the Psalms*,[2] and Kraus is a wonderfully helpful tool. But, whereas Kraus's treatment of the theology of the Psalms is essentially historically oriented, our approach is consciously *canonical*. We are not uninterested in the ancient Israelite views of God and humankind and the life of faith, but we are more interested in how the Psalms can speak to us in our time and place. We want to listen in on the conversation the Psalms wish to have with the claims of the Christian faith, and perhaps more suggestively with the claims of contemporary North American culture.

This chapter's title calls to mind the centerpiece of our American cultural heritage, "life, liberty, and the pursuit of happiness," as penned by Thomas Jefferson and trumpeted ever since as the clarion call of the good life to us all. So what will the contours of the conversation between the Psalms and our culture look like? The very first word of the very first Psalm is none other than happiness itself: "Happy are those . . . " We will see why this translation may make more sense than "Blessed are those . . . " The phrase also calls to mind Jesus' teaching in the Beatitudes: "Happy are the . . . " Just what is happiness after all? And how does the preacher weave a sermon on the subject in a way that answers the American pursuit, but in a theologically rich manner? In an interview in the *New York Times Magazine*, David Tracy characterized our task: "I wanted to think about religion and culture, and about these subjects in relationship to each other. Theology is what we call this attempt to think on religion culturally and on culture religiously."[3]

Let us analyze the persistent theme of "happiness" in our time. A rock artist from the boot heel of Missouri, Sheryl Crow, wrote a song titled "If It Makes You Happy," which has an intriguing refrain:

> If it makes you happy, it can't be that bad
> If it makes you happy, then why the hell are you so sad?

Crow says that she wrote this song "as a response to all the 'negative people' . . . [who] are incapable of finding or expressing true happiness." What exactly she meant is elusive. But her lyrics capture well what seems to be a pervasive reality of North American culture. We do and pursue what we *think* will make us happy, but we end up being "so sad." She had probably heard Mick Jagger's sentiment: "I can't get no satisfaction."

The Roman Catholic novelist Walker Percy eloquently characterized our dilemma by quoting another writer, John Cheever. As Cheever said, "The main emotion of the adult Northeastern American who has all the advantages of wealth, education, and culture is *disappointment*."

> Work is disappointing. . . . Marriage and family life are disappointing. . . . School is disappointing. . . . Politics is disappointing. . . . The churches are disappointing, even for most believers. If Christ brings us new life, it is all the more remarkable that the Church, the bearer of this good news, should be among the most dispirited institutions of the age.[4]

Disappointment! Mary Pipher warns of a crisis in our culture that erupts out of our pursuit of happiness as it simultaneously threatens our happiness:

> We have a crisis of meaning in our culture. The crisis comes from our isolation from each other, from the values we learn in a culture of consumption, and from the fuzzy, self-help message that the only commitment is to the self and the only important question is—Am I happy? We learn that we are number one and that our own immediate needs are the most important ones. The crisis comes from the message that products satisfy and that happiness can be purchased.[5]

The very existence of this crisis makes it crucial that we attend to and preach persuasively on the Psalms. For the *way* the Psalms teach us to pursue happiness is diametrically opposed to what our culture teaches.

Happy Are Those Who . . .

The very first word of the first Psalm is "Happy." James L. Mays has suggested that the rest of the book of Psalms can fruitfully be understood as a commentary on this one opening word, "Happy."[6]

> Happy are those
> who do not follow the advice of the wicked,
> or take the path that sinners tread,
> or sit in the seat of scoffers;
> but their delight is in the law of the LORD,
> and on [God's] law they meditate day and night. (Psalm 1:1-2)

To be sure, many have characterized this Psalmist as a boring, pedantic, self-righteous legalist. Consider the way Will Willimon opened a sermon on this text: "Here is someone whom you would not want for a roommate. Here is someone whom your mother might pick for your roommate. But even your mother wouldn't want to live next door to the person who wrote Psalm 1. Hell would be an entire Saturday night in the presence of this person."[7]

But we need to attend to the Psalm's countercultural perspective on happiness. The Hebrew word translated "law" is *Torah*, "instruction." Torah connotes not just instruction, but also movement, a way, an adventure toward a great destination. Psalm 1 portrays happiness as constant openness and attentiveness to God's instruction, or we could say, to God's will. This understanding of happiness is thoroughly God-centered, the very opposite of what our culture teaches us, that happiness derives from being self-centered.

The Psalm goes on to describe those who pursue happiness by opening themselves to God's instruction:

> They are like trees
> planted by streams of water,
> which yield their fruit in its season,
> and their leaves do not wither.
> In all that they do, they prosper. (Psalm 1:3)

This verse has frequently been misunderstood by those who detect here some sort of simplistic retributional scheme, especially when this verse is heard as an introduction to the rest of the Psalm, which concludes with the words:

> for the LORD watches over the way of the righteous,
> but the way of the wicked will perish. (Psalm 1:6)

The righteous prosper, the wicked perish—which makes God sound like a mechanical tit-for-tat potentate who gives all their just deserts. But the situation is more subtle and complex.

Mays has helped us to see that *prosper* in this Psalm does not mean to be rewarded for good behavior. Actually, the prosperity of the righteous consists of the connectedness of their lives to the life of God. Similarly, to *perish* does not mean to be punished but rather to live the sorry life that quite naturally results from cutting oneself off from God and God's instruction.[8] A better translation of Psalm 1:6 would be, "An evil life leads only to ruin."[9]

Autonomy and Wickedness

Psalm 1 at the same time invites us to a proper understanding of the key terms, *righteous* and *wicked*. The "righteous" are not the morally superior. The "righteous" are those who know that they live as a result of their connectedness to God. In other words, righteousness, according to Psalm 1, is anything but self-righteous legalism. It consists of humble openness to God and God's "instruction," or God's will, to be moving along God's path.

On the other hand, the "wicked" are not the obviously and outrageously bad folk. The "wicked" are those who claim to live on their own resources and resourcefulness. In short, if righteousness means to be thoroughly God-centered and God-directed, then wickedness means to be thoroughly self-centered and self-directed.

Or, to play off the term *law*, which is the traditional translation of *torah*, we could say that a synonym for wickedness is autonomy. The word *autonomy* is formed from the two Greek words, *autos* and *nomos*, "self" and "law." Autonomy, in its basic sense, means to be "a law unto oneself."

If there indeed is a crisis of meaning in our culture, perhaps we creatures who lunge for autonomy are the problem. From the perspective of Psalm 1, the entire Psalter, and indeed the whole Bible, autonomy is the essence of wickedness; and we live in a culture that promotes autonomy as a virtue and that systematically teaches us to be autonomous! To paraphrase the famous Pogo line, "We have seen the wicked, and it's us!"

The problem is deep-seated. To illustrate, let us turn from the field of biblical studies to the field of basketball. In 1993, when Michael Jordan "retired" from professional basketball to pursue baseball, his ex-boss summed up the situation in these words: "'It's like the American dream,' Bulls owner Jerry Reinsdorf said. 'The American dream is reaching a point in life where you don't have to do anything you don't want to do.'"[10]

Now, Jerry Reinsdorf is not a philosopher or a theologian, but he voiced the prevailing mind among us: The American Dream means reaching a point where you don't have to do anything you don't want to do! In other words, the American Dream means reaching a point in life where we can be totally self-centered, totally self-directed, and accountable to no one except ourselves.

The Irony of Independence

That the American Dream, our pursuit of happiness, has come to this should not be so surprising. After all, the phrase, "the pursuit of happiness," is from a document called "The Declaration of *Independence*." In a real sense, we've become so good at being independent and autonomous that we have no time for, nor much interest in, others. No time for God. No time for each other.

That's part of the problem that contributes to the current cultural crisis. As Mary Pipher put it, "The crisis comes from our *isolation* from each other."[11] This isolation needs no documentation. We sense it daily, hourly. Everybody knows that the institutions in our country are in trouble. They're in decline, both in terms of numbers and influence, and at all levels, families, schools, neighborhoods, churches, civic organizations. One of the most interesting assessments of the crisis is Robert Putnam's increasingly well-known essay titled "Bowling Alone: America's Declining Social Capital."[12] The title derives from the statistic that between 1980 and 1993 the number of people who bowled in the United States increased by 10 percent (to some 80 million people yearly in

1993). But during the same period, league bowling decreased by 40 percent. A lot more people are bowling alone! Now, Putnam admits that this statistic is whimsical, but of course, it's just one small part of a much larger trend that Putnam calls our "declining social capital" or our loss of "social connectedness," that which Pipher calls "our isolation from each other."

But that's only part of the problem. Pipher continued by saying that the crisis comes also "from the values we learn in a culture of consumption." Douglas Meeks has masterfully reminded us how capitalism, upon which we hang many fantasies of happiness, originally was derived from *theological* analysis.[13] The classical economists argued that when each person pursues his or her own self-interest, then the invisible hand of God, in the form of the market mechanism, balances out competing self-interests to the common good. According to this logic, one should be as greedy as one possibly can—for God's sake! The theory is flawed, of course. But plenty of those to whom we preach subscribe heartily to this doctrine. In the 1940s, Reinhold Niebuhr argued that "greed has become the besetting sin of a bourgeois culture."[14] Since Niebuhr's day, greed has run amok. What we learn in a culture of consumption is to be utterly selfish.

The whole North American situation, the pursuit of happiness along the paths of autonomy and greed, to borrow the words of Psalm 1:6, "leads only to ruin." Call it what you will—"disappointment," "declining social capital," "a crisis of meaning in our culture"—ruin is upon us. Niebuhr wrote a book in the early 1950s that dubbed this danger "the irony of American history."[15] Were he still living, he would no doubt want to update it by pointing out that democratic capitalism, which was established to enable our pursuit of happiness, is subtly leading us toward ruin. In a real sense, Mary Pipher has done this work of updating, when she points out the following. Here at the dawn of the new century,

> ironies abound. With more entertainment, we are bored. With more sexual information and stimulation, we experience less sexual pleasure. In a culture focused on feelings, people grow emotionally numb. With more time-saving devices, we have less time. With more books, we have fewer readers. With more mental health professionals, we have worse mental health.

Today we're in a more elusive crisis, a crisis of meaning, with emotional, spiritual and social aspects. We hunger for values, community and something greater than ourselves to dedicate our lives to. We wake in the night sorry for ourselves and our planet.[16]

Pipher's insights converge with those of Walker Percy concerning our pervasive disappointment: "We wake in the night sorry for ourselves and our planet." In other words, the American Dream is becoming a nightmare! Or, to paraphrase Psalm 1:6, "the way of the wicked is leading to our ruin."

Countercultural Enjoyment

Clearly, Psalm 1 and some of its key concepts can help us discern and articulate the nature and dimensions of the crisis of meaning in our culture. But how can the Psalms help us to confront the crisis constructively and respond faithfully? We have already hinted that Psalm 1 itself offers its portrayal of happiness that is thoroughly countercultural. Happiness does not derive from focusing upon ourselves and pursuing what we want. True happiness derives from constant attentiveness to God and the pursuit of what God may want for us and for our world.

This countercultural kind of happiness is what the Westminster Shorter Catechism calls "enjoying God," living into happiness by opening ourselves to God and following God's will. Nothing exposes the depth of our crisis more profoundly than the fact that the very notion of "enjoying God" seems nonsensical to most of us. We talk comfortably, almost mindlessly, about enjoying ourselves. But when does the enjoyment of God slide into conversation? The curiosity of the question reminds us of the scope of the alternative to autonomy and greed that could be ours through the first Psalm.

The Messiah

What Psalm 1 begins, Psalm 2 continues. Granted, the linkage may not be apparent at first sight, since Psalm 2 appears to be a portion of a liturgy that may have been used at the coronation of ancient Judean kings. The second verse of the Psalm mentions God's "anointed" (in Hebrew, *messiah*), the king. In verse 6, a voice, perhaps that of priest or prophet, announces on God's behalf: "I have set my king on Zion, my holy hill." To which the king responds:

> I will tell of the decree of the LORD:
> [God] said to me,
> "You are my son;
>   today I have begotten you."

According to Israel's theology of monarchy, the king was entrusted with the earthly enactment of God's will and was supposed to be nothing short of the earthly embodiment of God's purposes. Therefore, it is appropriate that Psalm 2 moves toward its conclusion with a voice, perhaps originally that of the new king, that invites the other kings and rulers of the earth to be "wise," to learn something. The king is cast in the role of *teacher*, and the remarkably simple but far-reaching lesson is this: "Serve the LORD with fear." "Serve" is a crucial word. Translated elsewhere as "worship," it means to submit to, to recognize the claim or sovereignty of, even to enslave oneself to. The king's lesson is a clear call to turn away from pursuing self-centered purposes and to pursue instead the purposes of God. Like Psalm 1, Psalm 2 ends with the warning that self-centered pursuits will "lead to ruin." "You will perish in the way" (2:12). And not surprisingly, the final line of Psalm 2 echoes the opening line of Psalm 1 by repeating the word "Happy": "*Happy* are all who take refuge in [God]."

Psalm 2's portrayal of happiness, like that of Psalm 1, is thoroughly *God*-centered. Happy are those who find their refuge (that is, their security, their strength, their meaning in life) in something or someone greater than themselves, something that cannot be purchased—in God! Both Psalms 1 and 2 sing of a profoundly countercultural understanding of happiness. So how do we thoroughly enculturated North Americans respond to this thoroughly countercultural invitation of Psalms 1 and 2?

Controller of Your Fate

The preacher should answer, and perhaps in two versions, one secular, the other more explicitly theological. Anne Lamott joins the chorus of voices noticing a crisis: "We are all in danger now and have a new everything to face, . . . My friend Carpenter says we no longer need Chicken Little to tell us the sky is falling, because it already has. The issue now is how to take care of one another."[17]

Well, there's one suggestion of what to do: Take care of one another. It sounds simple enough, but the real rub comes when we realize what this will involve. To take care of others means to yield control, to take ourselves out of the center, a remarkably difficult thing to do. As Lamott describes it:

> It helps to resign as the controller of your fate. All that energy we expend to keep things running right is not what's keeping things running right. We're bugs struggling in the river, brightly visible to the trout below. With that fact in mind, people like me make up all these rules to give us the illusion that we are in charge. I need to say to myself, they're not needed, hon. . . . Be kind to others, grab the fleck of riverweed, notice how beautifully your bug legs scull.[18]

If there is a particular heresy of North American Christianity, it is probably the perpetuation of the "illusion that we are in charge." In the Presbyterian Church (USA), for instance, at a time when all should humbly acknowledge that none of us knows what to do next and humbly listen for divine instruction for our place and time, we are busy making new rules—Proposition B, Proposition A, Proposition Whatever—all of it seems "to give us the illusion that we are in charge."

The Psalmists knew better. Anne Lamott, herself a Presbyterian, knows better: "It helps to resign as the controller of your fate." And to translate that message into its biblical-theological version, all we need to do is quote Mark 1:15: "The time is fulfilled, and the kingdom of God is at hand; repent, and believe in the good news." As Jesus announces the presence of the realm of God, he invites people to enter it. It won't be easy, because it means an about-face, a turnaround, a turning away from self-centeredness and an embrace of God's way (as in Psalm 1). And, then too, Jesus' announcement of the realm of God is essentially the same as what Psalm 2 proclaims: God's claim upon, God's sovereignty over the whole world.

It is not coincidental, of course, that Mark's Gospel opens by naming Jesus as "Christ" (*messiah*, "the anointed one") and "Son of God," both of which are featured in Psalm 2. Nor is it coincidental that Jesus' baptism in Mark 1:11 features a heavenly voice, whose stunning declaration is identical to what the divine voice says to the king in Psalm 2:6: "You are my son."

Jesus' fuller life and ministry recall Psalms 1 and 2. Specifically, the beginning of Jesus' teaching ministry in the Gospel of Matthew features the word "Happy." The Beatitudes stake out what happiness ultimately is about: "Happy are the poor in spirit . . . Happy are those who mourn . . . the meek . . . those who hunger and thirst for righteousness . . . the merciful . . . the pure in heart . . . the peacemakers . . . Happy are those who are persecuted for righteousness' sake." If you teach Sunday school in a congregation, you know that when the Beatitudes come up for consideration, someone will say, "That's not the real world!"

Real Reality

So true, yet so false. The world Jesus announces and describes, which we like to call the *real* "real world," is the realm of God. God's *real* world is constituted by God and by people who accept the invitation to resign as controllers of their fate. God's *real* world is sung in the Psalms, a world where happiness is pursued by constant orientation to God rather than self, where people are attentive to God's instruction and find "refuge" or security in God. God's *real* world is not the world of the American Dream, where autonomy results in ruinous isolation and rampant greed. That American Dream world is just that, a mere fantasy, a bogus pretender, a usurper that leaves us, as Sheryl Crow put it, "so sad."

A little later in the Sermon on the Mount, Jesus recalls Psalm 1 once more. In the Psalm there are two ways, one resulting in happiness and the other in ruin. Jesus also speaks of two roads, one that is easy but leads to destruction, the other that is hard but that leads to life (Matthew 7:13-14). This saying, so early in Jesus' ministry, anticipates the rest of his life and his death. Jesus would be constantly opposed; his "kingdom of nuisances and nobodies" (as John Dominic Crossan put it)[19] would be constantly ridiculed. Opposition and ridicule nailed Jesus to the cross.

Jesus' suffering, and the suffering to which he calls his followers with the invitation to pick up a cross and follow him (Mark 8:34), is, of course, another challenge to the American Dream. We'll talk more about that in the next chapter when we turn to the Psalms of lament. But for now, the good news from Psalms 1 and 2 and the Gospel of Jesus Christ is that life is possible and genuine happiness is possible, not in isolation from one another, and certainly not in what we can manage to purchase, but through our resignation as controllers of our fate to enter the realm of God, to stop deflecting the gracious gift God is literally dying to give us.

So now we turn to hear a sermon on another Torah Psalm, in this case Psalm 19. Some scholars have divided the Psalm into two, but we see an immense theological gain from construing the Psalm as a whole, tightly clasping the opening creation theme to that of the gift of the law in the second half.

The Smile on Duty's Face: A Sermon on Psalm 19

Perhaps the most famous remark from the German philosopher Immanuel Kant was: "Two things fill the mind with ever new and increasing admiration and awe, the oftener and more steadily we reflect upon them: the starry heavens above me and the moral law within me." Psalm 19 similarly combines a sense of awe over the grandeur of God's creation—something sadly lost on us moderns. We have cemented over much of God's world; there is so much phony, ambient light that we see a mere fuzzy trace of the skies the ancients contemplated. The whole praise of God for creation—that's another day, another sermon.[20]

Today we reflect upon the moral law—and, contrary to Kant, it is not within us. We do not emerge from the womb with some pre-wired morality. It comes from outside us. The Israelites left Egypt and wound up at Mount Sinai, where God gave Moses the law. And something in us just recoils when we think of "law" coming down from God. Like handcuffs stifling our desires, like going under the dentist's drill. Joe Heller imagines that when Moses came down with all those laws, his attorney popped out from behind a rock and said, "Uh, as your lawyer, I recommend we pore over the fine print before we finalize this deal."

But the Hebrew word translated "law" is *Torah*—and Torah is not some harsh directive tumbling from God's chisel. Torah means "way" or "path," and it implies movement, going somewhere. I love the Pasolini film, *The Gospel According to St. Matthew*. In it, Jesus is not like a statue, uttering timeless truths. Rather, he is on the move, in a hurry, the disciples breathlessly trying to keep up. On the way, he tells them things, and they have to remember them as they move on to the next task.

And to be going somewhere, somewhere meaningful, somewhere in sync with God—that is good. The God who wove together the immense yet intricate universe has created a way, a path. Without this Torah we are lost. Vaclav Havel said, "I believe that with the loss of God man has lost a kind of absolute and universal system of coordinates, to which he could always relate everything, chiefly himself. His world and his personality gradually began to break up into separate, incoherent fragments corresponding to different, relative coordinates." The Israelites understood. To them, the Torah was perfect, reviving the soul; it was more precious than gold, sweeter than honey.

Before she died, Mrs. Sarah Washam was our oldest church member, wily, opinionated, a gem. On my first visit with her, she suddenly said, "Do you know my favorite part of the Bible?" I said, "No, what's your favorite part of the Bible?" "The commandments!" was her surprising reply. "Why the commandments?" I had to ask. "Well, look at the mess the world's in. Don't you think we need the commandments?"

We may flinch over receiving our direction from outside ourselves. But there is nothing more liberating than the freedom of living in sync with the Creator of the entire universe, and of our very selves. Wordsworth said, "We know of nothing more beautiful than the smile on Duty's face." Robert E. Lee said, "Duty is the sublimest word in the English language."

To learn the way, to love Torah, requires disciplines, practice, training—as Psalm 1 suggests, "on his law we meditate day and night." My wife, Lisa, is an excellent seamstress. She begins with a pattern, then gathers her materials. The work is long, slow, with careful attention to detail. Sometimes there is some undoing, then redoing. A smocked dress, not made in a night, in the end is a thing of beauty. So it is with the virtuous life. There is a pattern; and the progress is slow, requiring energy, detail, some undoing, some redoing.

I've tried to put together some examples from the Torah, from God's pattern. The Ten Commandments tell us, "Remember the Sabbath day to keep it holy." Some of us can remember when Sunday was a sour day. Now it's fair game for any and everything. But God made us increasingly burnt-out people in such a way that we desperately need rest, and we need to worship God.

"Thou shalt not kill." Most of us have avoided murder. But Jesus, in the Sermon on the Mount, had this annoying habit of cutting through to the heart of such matters. He said, Well, if you've been angry, it's the same. Now it's not that Jesus decided to have a rule that it's bad to get angry. It's that he wants us to be set free from our anger. Augustine said that anger directed at another person is like a sword, but it must first pass through our own heart before going at the other. Anger consumes and devastates us.

We live in a sexually crazed culture. But the Bible suggests that there are secrets of intimacy reserved for those in a lifelong commitment—and not because God is a spoilsport who would deny us pleasure. Rather, there is a higher pleasure, a deeper joy, when our intimacy isn't spread around so thin.

Jesus said, "Love your enemies." Otto von Bismarck said you cannot run a country based on the Sermon on the Mount. But this past Thursday was the "National Day of Prayer," and I should imagine that all over this country people prayed "God bless America." But if we dare ask for God's "blessing," we really have to be serious about forming our lives according to what Jesus taught us. Love your enemies. Do not lay treasure up for yourself on earth. The law of the Lord is more precious than gold.

But my main focus for the moment is on what I regard as Jesus' most un-obeyed commandment. "When you give a dinner party, do not invite those who are able to invite you back, but invite the poor, the maimed, the lame, the blind." Now, you know how to do dinners, how to go out, make reservations, wear the right clothes, study the menu, banter with the waiter, lift the proper fork. You know how to host dinners, with appetizers, the right number of chairs, some after-dinner conversation and coffee. But have you invited anyone who is poor? Anyone who is black? Anyone who is maimed, hurt by the world in some way?

We are always pitching mission opportunities at you—and some of you respond, and with great energy. But you can't just scratch your head and think, "Well, that doesn't suit my schedule," or "I'll wait for something more convenient." Serving the poor is not just some good idea that may make you feel good, a nice option if you aren't already too busy. It is in the pattern, it is where Jesus is going, if we wish to keep up. Serving the poor is part of that *Torah* that revives the soul, is more precious than gold, sweeter than honey. And I know you have the brains, the creativity, to figure out how to serve the poor. If you can plan great summer vacations, with proper reservations and attire and travel schedule, I just know you can apply yourself and follow Christ on this exciting "way."

We have a new habit as a staff when we go out to lunch. It started when Andy came as our new associate. The first time I took him to the Rainbow Deli, the waitress came up and said, "Hi, I'm Jennifer, and I'll be your waitress today." Andy warmly sends back his own introduction: "Well, hi, I'm Andy, and this is James, and we'll be your customers today." I do this all the time now, introducing everybody at the table. Some of the waitresses think I'm crazy. And I tell them I mean it only in good fun.

But maybe it shouldn't just be for fun. A few years ago we brought Bishop Kenneth Goodson, one of our most eloquent preachers this century, to Charlotte to speak at an event. There was a dinner beforehand. Everything began normally enough. The waitress came, collected orders, brought drinks, and finally served their meals. After she laid down the last plate, Bishop Goodson grasped her hand and said, "We're about to have a prayer here. Won't you join us?" She said okay. And so he prayed. "Lord, thank you for this day, for the church, for your Son Jesus. Thank you for this food . . . " And so forth. Then he wound up his prayer by saying, "And, Lord, we thank you for this beautiful waitress, for her smile, for the kind way she has served us. And, Lord, if she has any need, if there is any hardship in her life, just bless her, and love her." After he said "Amen," there were tears streaming down her face. She said, "How did you know I was hurting today?" He said, "I didn't know." But he did. And you and I know. Every person we brush up against during the day is hurting. They are all lonely; they want to be touched, to belong, to be ushered into the presence of God.

Look up at the starry heavens, the sun and moon. Their courses are governed by the God who did not just etch commandments on some lifeless stone in millennia gone by. Those commandments are woven into the very fabric of creation, into the purpose for your life. Receive with joy, treasure them above finest gold, delight in them more than honey. And practice. Especially at the dinner party.

CHAPTER 7

The Problem of Pain

Having delved into Psalms 1 and 2 in the previous chapter, we move forward to Psalm 3, an instructive sample of the Psalms of lament or complaint. And again we will place this Psalm in conversation with our culture. On their CD, *Automatic for the People*, REM has a song titled "Everybody Hurts." Naturally there is a video version; as the group sings words like "Everybody hurts . . . everybody cries sometimes," the video depicts the pained faces of persons in cars that are tied up in traffic on a freeway, a too familiar symbol of isolation and alienation (and nowadays rage). Suddenly, one of the pained individuals makes a decision. He gets out of his car. Others get out of their cars, and a community of mutual support spontaneously forms right in the middle of the highway. The leading voice sings: "It's time to sing along . . . no, no, you are not alone." An unlikely scenario—and its very unlikeliness helps to make the point.

The preacher may recognize that "Everybody Hurts" envisions the essential movement we find in the Psalter's laments, that dramatic movement from lament to praise or assurance, from "everything is wrong" to "you are not alone." And, as the video suggests, this movement is no mere coincidence. At the crucial moment when the man gets out of his car, a graphic at the bottom of the screen reads: "Lead me to the rock that is higher than I." Imagine: a Bible verse, from a lament (Psalm 61:2), featured in an REM video! Moments later another graphic appears: "They that sow in tears shall reap in joy." Another Bible verse, this one from Psalm 126, another Psalm of lament.

The traffic image, which overlies the lyrics, yet juxtaposed with words of Scripture, is a profound and accurate rendering of the human situation as portrayed in the Psalms. Everybody hurts. Even the righteous folks in the Psalter regularly find themselves in the midst of situations where "everything is wrong." Yet remember that in Psalms 1 and 2, the "righteous" are said to be "happy."

Perhaps, as we discern the Psalms for preaching, we face the herculean task of helping our listeners to understand that happiness is not incompatible with suffering.

Something Is Really Wrong

This is no easy task in our culture that systematically tries to teach us that suffering and pain are aberrations. It is abnormal to hurt. Pain is to be avoided at all cost. If you cannot avoid pain, you deny it. If you cannot avoid or deny it, then at least go out and buy something to make yourself feel better. And if what Anne Lamott calls "retail therapy" doesn't work, then there is something really wrong—with you.[1]

To be tutored by such a culture is deadly, literally deadly in all too many cases. We'll come back to this lethality, but for now, let us consider the way Psalm 3 presents the *normal* situation of those whom Psalms 1 and 2 called "happy." Entering into Psalm 3, the first actual prayer directed to God in the Psalms, we cannot fail to notice that the Psalmist *hurts*.

> O LORD, how *many* are my foes!
> *Many* are rising against me;
> *many* are saying to me,
> "There is no help for you in God."

Many, many, many. The Psalmist is surrounded by opposition. Notice too that what these many *say* identifies them as defiantly *autonomous*, which Psalm 1 suggested to be the essence of wickedness. "There is no help for you in God." In other words, if you're going to make it, you'll have to make it *on your own*, by your*self*. The "many" directly contradict the wisdom of Psalm 2, "Happy are all who take refuge in God."

What is frightening is that most of us North Americans sense that there is no help for us in God. Do not believe for one moment that everyone to whom you preach is full of faith in God's help. Plenty scratch their heads and wonder in the darkness. And plenty of others unwittingly deny God's help by twisting what the Gospel is about. Americans love to say, "God helps those who help themselves." Many people actually believe this is in the Bible somewhere. The origin of this pithy saying is most certainly not the

Bible, but rather *Poor Richard's Almanack*. However much we admire the resourcefulness and pluck of Benjamin Franklin, if we really believe that God helps those who help themselves, then we need not talk about God at all. We certainly need not open our Bibles, where we find a God who would not prove congenial to cynics like Franklin. Just help yourself. And so we do, or at least we try to. The bookshelves are weighed down with tons of self-help literature to help us help ourselves.

I Only Pray When I'm in Trouble

But the Psalmist refuses to believe what the many, what the crowds, say. The Psalmist knows and trusts that God helps those who can*not* help themselves. Instead of marshalling his own resources, the Psalmist prays, "Help me, O my God!" (3:7 author translation). Then we hear a simple, profound affirmation of faith: "Help belongs to the LORD" (v. 8 author translation).

Everybody hurts, everything is wrong, many are my foes—but help belongs to the Lord, and you are not alone. In the midst of all that is wrong, this Psalmist can "lie down and sleep, [and] wake again" in the assurance that "the LORD sustains me" (v. 5). In other words, contentment, security, happiness are all possible, not merely after or beyond the suffering, but in the very throes of suffering.

Isaac Bashevis Singer once said, "I only pray when I'm in trouble; but I'm in trouble all the time."[2] In trouble all the time! That's "normal" for the Psalmists, and for the preacher and those who listen to preachers. Psalm 3 is a typical lament, hardly alone. We find seventy or eighty more laments in the Psalter. The laments, these cries in distress from those who cannot help themselves, are the dominant voice in the book. The astonishing truth is that these dozens of pleas (with one possible exception, Psalm 88), *all* move from complaint to assurance, a movement we analyzed in chapter 5.

But do not misconstrue this movement. We do not mean that the arrival at assurance or praise means that suffering has been left behind. Quite the contrary! For the Psalmists, happiness and suffering are not opposites, but rather they always coexist. As Mays puts it, commenting on another of the laments (Psalm 13): "The agony and the ecstasy belong together as the secret of our identity."[3] That the agony and the ecstasy, that suffering and happiness, *belong together* has profound theological importance. Preachers must shout this elusive truth from the rooftop and hold the hurting hands of their parishioners while explaining two crucial implications of this surprising but hopeful word.

Retribution Dismantled

First, if suffering and happiness belong together, then suffering cannot be interpreted as divine punishment. Psalm 34:19 states it clearly: "Many are the afflictions of the righteous." To be sure, there are places in the Psalms that seem to articulate a doctrine of retribution, that the good are materially rewarded and the wicked are punished. Psalm 38, for instance, begins:

> O LORD, do not rebuke me in your anger,
>   or discipline me in your wrath.
> For your arrows have sunk into me,
>   and your hand has come down on me.

> There is no soundness in my flesh
>   because of your indignation;
> there is no health in my bones
>   because of my sin.

But the rest of the Psalm hints that the Psalmist views his or her suffering not as an unambiguous sign of condemnation but rather as something that will evoke God's compassion.

In other Psalms it is very explicit that the Psalmist has done nothing wrong or sinful to cause the suffering that she or he is experiencing. In several Psalms, the prayer for help is accompanied by a so-called protestation of innocence. We may paraphrase Psalm 7:3-5: "O LORD, if there is wrong in my hands, then go ahead and really trample me into the dust!" In other words, "I swear I'm innocent."

Not coincidentally, Psalm 7 reminds us of the book of Job. Job's suffering was also undeserved and *not* indicative of divine punishment. In short, the book of Psalms, like the book of Job, also confronts the issue of *theodicy*, the question of how God could be just, given the sufferings of the innocent; or as we ask today, "Why do bad things happen to good people?" Like the book of Job, the Psalter answers this haunting question by obliterating the doctrine of retribution.[4] The consequences of a rigid doctrine of retribution cannot be underestimated. Wendy Farley described it provocatively:

> One of the most terrible beliefs of Christianity is that God punishes us with suffering. It is a belief inflicted on grief-stricken or pain-ridden individuals to justify their suffering and on groups to justify their continued oppression. The association of suffering with punishment denies even the right to resist suffering. . . . Further, this sadistic theology conspires with pain to lock God away from the sufferer, for whom God becomes the ostensibly righteous torturer. The love of God is gone, and the pious sufferer is betrayed into the hands of despair. This is the theology of Job's "comforters," who heap despair onto suffering by trying to show that God, too, has turned against the sufferer.[5]

Suffering is not to be justified. Suffering happens. God is no sadist, doling out a car crash here, a melanoma there. And God most certainly refuses to be locked away from the one who suffers, but is most intensely present in the midst of suffering. The sermon on Psalm 72 will say more on this issue.

The Origin of Suffering

There is another theological implication. We may ask: If suffering is not doled out by God, then how do we explain its origin? The Psalms suggest a partial answer, which is "the wicked." Those who refuse God's direction toward justice and righteousness, those who choose their own selfish way—these folk are responsible for introducing destructive and oppressive dynamics into the human situation that lead to the suffering of other people. Obviously we bring plenty of suffering on ourselves, and on others.[6] But there is more to this, something strange and unspeakably deep. We human beings not only have the freedom to inflict suffering on ourselves and on others. We also have the tragic ability to inflict suffering upon God!

God suffers. However much we may prefer an omnipotent, sanitized God aloof from all suffering, the God of the Psalms, and of the entire Bible, is a God who suffers. Not only do the righteous have enemies that cause them to suffer, but God also has enemies that cause God to suffer. Don't forget that in Psalm 2, nations and peoples and their kings and rulers line up *against God* as well as against God's anointed. So, when Psalm 2 affirms God's sovereign power, we are drawn to construe power in a very particular way. God's power does not overwhelm any and all foes, but actually permits the existence of opposition! The proper term to characterize God's kind of power is not *force*, as we usually think of power. Rather, the proper name for this kind of power is *love*. Thus, the crucial corollary to the truth that God suffers is this: that God's power, the force behind the universe, is *love!*[7] From this perspective, suffering, human suffering *and* God's suffering, is to be viewed essentially as a condition for participation in a universe where the fundamental reality is love. Anyone who has ever loved knows this truth, usually through painful experience.

Thus for the Psalmist, this curious coexistence of suffering and happiness ultimately means that in this universe, as God has created it, to live and to love will mean to suffer. Suffering will be a sign of one's loving involvement in and with the lives of others as well as one's involvement with God. It is precisely here that the theology of the Psalms so desperately needs to be heard in our culture. The Psalms can help us to realize that our loss of "social connectedness," our failure to care for each other, is inextricably linked to our pervasive tendency to avoid suffering at all cost. And the Psalms can teach us the futility of trying to pretend that we can or should try to avoid suffering, a lesson we desperately need to learn, perhaps before it is forced upon us.

Better than Monday Morning

We spend millions of dollars every day in this country trying to convince ourselves that suffering is an aberration. We call it *advertising*. According to Mary Pipher, "Advertising teaches that people shouldn't have to suffer, that pain is unnatural and can be cured."[8] Wryly, but accurately enough, she calls the USA "the United States of *Advertising*"![9] Advertising certainly is effective. Not only do we buy the products we see and hear advertised, but we also buy the underlying message that pain is unnatural and to be avoided, denied, or at least compensated for by purchasing more stuff.

But since stuff is nothing but stuff, and cannot satisfy the yearn-
ings of our souls, then the effect of buying into this culture is
deadly. When we parents, and the advertisers and the television,
teach our children that pain is unnatural and abnormal, they will
often have few emotional or spiritual resources to deal with the
pain and suffering that are part of being human. Rampant suicide
rates among teenagers must have something to do with our culture's pervasive teaching that pain is abnormal. All too often, when
our young people are hurting, they are left to conclude that there's
something terribly wrong with themselves and that life must not
be worth living, and they act accordingly. The song and video,
"Everybody Hurts," has been adopted for use in teen suicide pre-
vention campaigns, and such use is a concrete illustration of how
what the Psalms teach may help us to reorient ourselves and our
culture.

Even for those who don't die, who survive to soak up yet
another day in our media culture, there is still a deadening as we
are numbed to the experience of what the Psalms call "happiness,"
and with devastating results. Because advertising and television
programming teach us that life should be not merely pain-free but
also constantly exciting, glamorous, and entertaining, we hardly
know how to deal with the ordinariness of everyday life. Because
mundane reality is not exciting enough, we escape into "virtual
reality." Virtual reality may seem harmless enough, but it may give
us pause to consider the number and variety of bizarre, dangerous,
and deadening ways we vainly attempt to cope with what we perceive to be the dull ache of the ordinariness of daily living.

In *The Last Gentleman*, Walker Percy's main character, Will
Barrett, describes his father's "happiness" on the day Pearl Harbor
was bombed:

> On the days of bad news there was the same clearing and sweet-
> ness in the air. Azaleas could be seen. He remembered his father's
> happiness when he spoke of Pearl Harbor—where he was when
> he heard it, how he had called the draft board the next morning.
> It was not hard to see him walking to work on that Monday. For
> once the houses, the trees, the very cracks in the sidewalk had not
> their usual minatory presence. The dreadful threat of weekday
> mornings was gone! War is better than Monday morning.[10]

When war is better than Monday morning, we have lost all ability to discern and experience happiness. Little wonder depression is so rampant, as we drown in the malaise of a life that can never maintain scintillating levels in the face of routines, aging, and plain old boredom, not to mention the specter of suffering and death that can never be banished. Pipher is right when she says "almost all the craziness in the world comes from running from pain."[11]

Christianity and the Lament

The Christian faith, despite a certain politeness that seems to threaten our full use of the lament,[12] has appropriated through its use of the Psalms this sense that "everybody hurts," that suffering is not far from God, but is as near as God's own heart. We saw previously how Psalms 1 and 2 influenced the Gospel accounts of Jesus' early ministry. Even more directly, the laments have shaped the stories of Jesus, especially as we approach the gruesome end of Jesus' ministry, his passion, death, and resurrection.

In fact, the three longest and most intense of the laments, Psalms 22, 31, and 69, figure prominently in the Gospels. "My God, my God, why have you forsaken me?" is the opening of Psalm 22. This very question becomes Jesus' poignant question from the cross (in Matthew and Mark). The details of the Psalmist's suffering in Psalm 22 become the threads woven into the tapestry of the crucifixion scene in the Gospels. The Psalmist and Jesus are mocked, their garments divided by the casting of lots. Luke's Gospel omits the cry of dereliction, "My God, my God, why have you forsaken me?" Instead, Luke relates that from the cross, Jesus prays, "Into your hands I commend my spirit," the familiar words from Psalm 31:5. And Psalm 69 supplies the detail of Jesus being offered vinegar to drink.

For the moment we may bracket a host of historical and literary questions on how the Psalms wound up being used in the Gospels. Instead we will make a *canonical* point. The *effect* of the Gospel writers' use of the Psalms of lament to narrate the story of Jesus' passion is to present Jesus as the ultimate fulfillment, or even paradigm of the faithful Psalmist, who suffers brutally, even chronically, but who simultaneously finds refuge or happiness in God. So we see that Jesus gives fullest expression to the two theological implications we identified earlier. First, Jesus' suffering as a human being is clearly not divine punishment. And second, because Jesus is the incarnation of God, Jesus' suffering embodies the very suffering of God, demonstrating concretely that the power of God is ultimately manifest as sacrificial love.

The convergence of this cruciform demonstration with the Beatitudes is clear. Those whom Jesus pronounced "happy" are precisely those who regularly are identified as the pray-ers of the Psalms of lament: the humble, the meek, the poor, the needy, and the persecuted. When the pray-ers hurt, they simultaneously find refuge in God; they are "happy," as Jesus also proclaimed and made reality. When the church actually embraces and embodies this message, the results are revolutionary. For instance, to state it sort of negatively first, we show our culture what it means to avoid the deadening effects and the craziness that come from running from pain. More positively to grasp the good news that the agony and ecstasy belong together can instill in us what H. H. Schmid has called "courage for the fragmentary."[13] To live in the realm of God where happiness is a reality in the midst of pain and suffering would, in Schmid's words, "free us from dogged striving toward the realization of the ultimate righteousness at any cost and from the frustration that necessarily arises from it." In other words, understanding that suffering and joyful hope belong together would free us from "burnout," from disappointment and despair. This "courage for the fragmentary" would make Monday mornings bearable, and even joyful.

Then there is this. If suffering should not be interpreted as divine punishment, then neither can prosperity be interpreted as divine reward. Or, to put it theologically, only when the doctrine of retribution is destroyed does *grace* become a meaningful concept. By obliterating the doctrine of retribution, the Psalms of lament ultimately invite us to live by grace. And when we live by grace, the revolutionary result will be a wonderfully genuine "solidarity" among all kinds of people because no one considers him or herself or their group better than anyone else.[14]

Take note of this "solidarity" in the case of the sufferer of Psalm 35. Responding to the suffering of others, the Psalmist says:

> But as for me, when they were sick
> > I wore sackcloth;
> > I afflicted myself with fasting.
> I prayed with head bowed on my bosom,
> > as though I grieved for a friend or brother;
> I went about as one who laments for a mother,
> > bowed down and in mourning.

The prayer of the Psalm persists in this posture despite the fact that others do not treat him or her this way when he or she suffers. Such "solidarity" we could call simply "love." And nothing is more endangered, nothing more desperately needed, in a culture governed by the logic of autonomy, than love.

Next is a sermon on Psalm 22, a text we associate almost exclusively with the lonely suffering of Jesus, but the sermon explores the way that suffering brings us into solidarity with God and also with the most surprising people.

A Sermon on Psalm 22

Very late at night when I can't manage to read or write another word about the Psalms but am still wide awake, I read novels.[15] One of my all-time favorites is titled *Littlejohn*; it's by Howard Owen, who of all things is the sports editor for the *Richmond [Virginia] Times Dispatch*. The narrator for most of the book is Litttlejohn, an elderly eastern North Carolina farmer who looks back over his life as he prepares to die. At one point, he's recalling his military service traveling through Germany at the very end of World War II:

> It's queer to me now to hear Georgia [my daughter] talk about how warm and friendly European people are. She goes on vacation over there every chance she gets, and she can't get enough of it. To me, it was a place where God didn't live. Oh, I know God is everywhere, but maybe sometimes, in some places, He leaves for a while just to see what happens while He's gone, or maybe just to test folks like He did Job. There must have been all kinds of people of France and Germany and England that looked up in the sky full of bombs and hopelessness and asked, "My God, why have you forsaken me?"
> There was times, on that long trip into Germany, and espe-

cially after we knew what the Nazis had done, when it passed through me like a knife that the devil might be winning, that the whole world might be lost.[16]

"My God, my God, why have you forsaken me?" It's an old, old question that is chillingly contemporary. It was the ancient Psalmist's question in the midst of some terrible distress. It was Jesus' question from the cross. As Littlejohn points out, it is certainly the question of those caught in the horrors of hostility and warfare. And as you and I look out upon the world or the church or our own lives, it is *our question* as well; for it often appears "that the whole world might be lost."

The names have changed: Bosnians and Serbs, Irish Catholics and Irish Protestants. But people are still killing each other in Europe and in other places as well, including regularly on the streets of my town and yours. "My God, my God, why have you forsaken us?"

Not too long ago, right here in the United States, a Baptist church voted unanimously to deny membership to a new couple who wanted to join the church. Why? Because they were African American, and the church was all white. "My God, my God, why have you forsaken us?"

I don't know all your problems; in fact, I'm not even sure I know all mine. But the ones I *am* aware of are of such magnitude from time to time to make it seem as if the whole world, as I know it at least, might be lost. I find myself joining my voice with that of the Psalmist and Jesus and multitudes of believers throughout the centuries who have taken up Psalm 22 as their prayer, "My God, my God, why have you forsaken me?" Perhaps this is your prayer too!

The remarkable thing about Psalm 22, though, is not that it is such an eloquent expression of the perennial human experience of suffering and God-forsakenness. Rather, the truly remarkable thing is that it doesn't stop there. Verse 2 asks God to answer, and verse 21*b* affirms that an answer has come. Literally, verse 21*b* reads: "From the horns of the wild oxen, you (God) have answered me." It seems a little strange, so strange in fact that the translators of the NRSV felt compelled to use *rescued* from the horns of the wild oxen, but the Hebrew certainly seems to suggest that the "answer" to the Psalmist's terrible distress involves the assurance that God does not despise or abhor the affliction of the afflicted (v. 24). The

Psalmist comes to realize that even in the midst of suffering, *especially* in the midst of suffering, God is present. God *shares* the affliction of the afflicted. God suffers too.

To be sure, this answer is not the easy answer the world is generally looking for any more than the cross was the answer that Jesus' disciples were looking for. We'd prefer a God who fixes everything, but the use of Psalm 22 in the New Testament suggests that the cross of Jesus reveals a God *who shares our affliction*. For the Psalmist, though, this answer is more than sufficient. Indeed, the assurance that God does not despise the affliction of the afflicted makes all the difference in the world!

The Psalmist's complaint can be accompanied by praise. Verse 25: "From you comes my praise in the great congregation." And the Psalmist apparently shows gratitude to God with a thank-offering of a sacrificial animal, portions of which were shared at a celebratory meal with whomever the Psalmist invited. And *whom* does the Psalmist invite? Those who also are afflicted! Verse 26: "The poor shall eat and be satisfied." Actually, the Psalmist envisions that the families of the nations will somehow be there! Even the dead and the yet-unborn will somehow participate.

If all this sounds familiar, it should. Just as the Psalmist's opening words anticipate Jesus' suffering and death, so the Psalmist's concluding actions anticipate Jesus' whole life and ministry, as well as his resurrection. Jesus' entire earthly ministry was a prolonged and emphatic demonstration that God does not despise the afflicted. Indeed, as the reading from Mark 2 indicated, Jesus invited the despised to be his followers. He ate with the poor and the outcast and the afflicted. Jesus' humiliating death reinforced the message: God does not despise the afflicted. Rather, God *shares* their affliction. And right before he died, Jesus told his followers to keep on eating together as a sign of thanksgiving for the good news. We call it Eucharist (thanksgiving) or Communion or the Lord's Supper.

For me, one of the holiest, most meaningful days of the Christian year, right up there with Easter and Christmas is World Communion Sunday. For on that day, we worship together, we eat together, explicitly reminding ourselves that our gathering and our table include the whole world—Americans, Europeans, Africans, and Asians; black and white and red and yellow; rich and poor—*all* together, no one, no group any better than any other.

There's a word that describes this kind of gathering: love! How interesting, and hardly coincidental, that Psalm 23 ends like Psalm 22 does—with the Psalmist at a table, hosted by, as one hymn puts it, "The King of Love." *Others* are there as well, friends, we assume, but also *enemies*! And precisely when *all* are so gathered, the Psalmist realizes and proclaims that "surely goodness and mercy (i.e., God's unfailing love) will *pursue* me all the days of my life."

When we afflicted ones gather, and when, as the Psalmist and as Jesus did, we invite the whole world, then I know that apparent God-forsakenness is never the final word. When we gather, all of us, as the Psalmist and as Jesus invited us to do, life and love are palpable realities, and then I know that evil is *not* winning, and then I know that the world is not lost.

The same Psalmist who began with the haunting question, "My God, my God, why have you forsaken me?" concludes his meal, shared with all the world's afflicted, with a simple promise: "I shall live for God." The Psalmist invites us to do the same. Thanks be to God. Amen.

CHAPTER 8

The Cause for Celebration

We see plenty of celebrations in our world. A ticker tape parade takes place in New York after the Yankees win the pennant. Applause breaks out as a young man and woman cut a towering white wedding cake. A dozen children wearing party hats squeal as the candles are blown out. Fireworks light up the summer sky on Independence Day. Coworkers and friends roast one entering retirement.

But perhaps our most superficially theological celebration in America is Thanksgiving. Seemingly a time for Americans to express their gratitude to God, Thanksgiving instead becomes an extravaganza of overindulgence. Reinhold Niebuhr, after attending a community Thanksgiving service in Detroit in 1927, told the hard truth:

> Thanksgiving becomes increasingly the business of congratulating the Almighty upon his most excellent co-workers, *ourselves* . . . The Lord who was worshiped was not the Lord of Hosts, but the spirit of Uncle Sam, given a cosmic eminence for the moment which the dear old gentleman does not deserve.[1]

More recently, Walter Brueggemann has pointed out how easily the theology of praise in the Psalms can become the ideology of the proud, the prosperous, and the powerful as they attempt to maintain the *status quo*.[2] Given our discussion in chapter 6, we may notice how Brueggemann speaks of praise as "lyrical self-abandonment,"[3] in which case praise is the antithesis of congratulating ourselves. Praise subverts the *status quo*, particularly the kind of "normalcy" that places me and my comfortable existence squarely at the center of the universe. The God praised so eloquently in the Psalms is not the guarantor of the American Dream, which proffers nothing more than a hollow salvation accrued through work, maybe even through luck, and most certainly through consumption. We ignore Niebuhr's and Brueggemann's warnings at our peril.

Revelation and Celebration

To pay heed, we must appreciate and appropriate the songs of praise and thanksgiving as both *celebration* and *revelation*. Our hunger for celebration is captured in another song from Sheryl Crow, "Hard to Make a Stand." God sneaks into the lyrics:

> We got loud guitars and quiet suspicions . . .
> And we still argue over who is God.

The Psalms of praise, in poetic, musical form, present their lyrical argument about God, a God who well knows the need expressed at the end of Crow's song: "We all need a celebration."

On the CD she sings "celebration"; but the printed lyrics sheet reads "We all need a *revelation*." Biblical scholars would call this a text-critical problem. We even wonder if this is a modern example of the phenomenon called *kethibh-qere*, where the original Hebrew text (the *kethibh*, what is "written") is marked with a little circle above the word, pointing you to the margin where we find another word, the one to be said out loud (the *qere*, what is "read").[4] A little research unearths the fact that Sheryl Crow has recorded three versions of this song, one ending with "We all need a celebration," one with "We all need a revelation," and one ending with both.

This ambivalence is theologically provocative, capturing an elusive truth little understood nowadays. The songs of praise in the Psalms are both celebration and revelation. And when we attend carefully to what they reveal or teach, then we will not stumble into the mistake of using expressions of praise to celebrate our own good fortune or to congratulate ourselves for our ingenuity and hard work. Indeed, we shall discover that the songs of praise are particularly timely and well-suited for reaching and teaching us folk who are tempted to conclude that we of "the 'I want' generation"[5] can buy whatever we want, even salvation. We need a celebration that is simultaneously a revelation.

Let us look at a song of praise and thanksgiving that very explicitly invites the reader to hear and appropriate its words as revelation along with the celebration. Psalm 100 voices six invitations to celebration:

> Make a joyful noise . . .
>> Worship the LORD with gladness, . . .
> come into his presence with singing. . . . .
> Enter his gates with thanksgiving . . .
> Give thanks to him,
> bless his name.

The first three of these invitations come in verses 1-2, and the final three come in verse 4. Situated right in the middle of them (verse 3) we are called to attend to some revelation:

> *Know* that the LORD is God.
>> It is he that made us, and we are his.
>> We are his people, and the sheep of his pasture.

This extraordinarily simple affirmation is simply extraordinary in our kind of culture: "We belong to God." Autonomy is a perversion of the truth of reality. The Psalm subverts all the racket of our world that would dupe us into believing that we can buy anything we really need. So simple is this affirmation that we may miss its radical edge. Remember the corollary to "We belong to God," which is "We are not our own." The apostle Paul tells the Corinthians, "You are not your own" (1 Corinthians 6:19), just as he summons them to glorify God. Brian Wren has written a hymn, "We Are Not Our Own," that beautifully articulates the revelation of Psalm 100. Its first and last stanzas are:

> We are not our own.
> Earth forms us, human leaves
> on nature's growing vine.
> Fruit of many generations,
> seeds of life divine.

> Let us be a house of welcome,
> living stone upholding living stone,
> Gladly showing all our neighbors,
> we are not our own![6]

Are you rattled by the clash of Wren's hymn against the noise of our culture whose message is "it's my life to live"? The relief the Psalmist offers us is that our lives are *not* simply ours to live, because "We belong to God." And unless we know that our lives are not our own, we open ourselves to the logic of autonomy and to its inevitable results, ruinous isolation and rampant greed, not to mention exhaustion.

The Meaning of Life

When pastors ask people to use just one adjective to describe how they are, the predominant answer is, "I am tired." Autonomous people are exhausted because, like Sisyphus, they toil alone, rolling a huge stone up some hill, a hill with no reachable summit. Or perhaps a better mythological metaphor would be that we are like Atlas, hoisting the whole world on our shoulders. However gamely we struggle, the world finally crushes us.

Scott Peck shares part of a conversation between himself and one of his clients, Charlene:

> "Everything seems meaningless," Charlene complained to me one day.
>
> What is the meaning of life?" I asked her with seeming innocence.
>
> "How should I know?" she replied with obvious irritation.
>
> "You're a dedicated religious person," I responded. "Surely your religion must have something to say about the meaning of life."
>
> "You're trying to trap me," Charlene countered.
>
> "That's right," I acknowledged. "I am trying to trap you into seeing your problem clearly. What does your religion hold to be the meaning of life?"
>
> "I am not a Christian," Charlene proclaimed. "My religion speaks of love, not of meaning."
>
> "Well, what do Christians say as to the meaning of life? Even if it isn't what you believe, at least it's a model."
>
> "I'm not interested in models."
>
> "You were raised in the Christian Church. You spent almost two years as a professional teacher of Christian doctrine," I went on . . . "Surely you're not so dumb as to be unaware of what Christians say is the meaning of life, the purpose of human existence."

"We exist for the glory of God," Charlene said in a flat, low monotone, as if she were sullenly repeating an alien catechism, learned by rote and extracted from her at gunpoint. "The purpose of our life is to glorify God." [Obviously, she was raised as a Presbyterian!]

"Well?" I asked.

There was a short silence. For a brief moment I thought she might cry—the one time in our work together. "I cannot do it. There's no room for *me* in that. That would be my death," she said in a quavering voice. Then, with a suddenness that frightened me, what seemed to be her choked-back sobs turned into a roar. "I don't want to live for God. I will not. I want to live for me. My own sake!"

It was another session in the middle of which Charlene walked out. I felt a terrible pity for her. I wanted to cry, but my own tears would not come. "Oh God, she's *so alone*," was all I could whisper.[7]

The tragic irony is that when we pursue the logic of autonomy, when we think that we are our own, then we end up so very alone.

J. California Cooper has a short story titled "Friends, Anyone?" in which the main character relentlessly pursues everything she wants, only to realize after she has grown older that she is utterly isolated. In desperation, she seeks companionship, a friend, *anyone*; but her only acquaintances are all just like her. Cooper describes them:

They drank together, but seldom looked at each other unless along with a snide remark. Their faces were turned away from their own table toward the rest of the crowded, busy room. Looking, seeking.

All each *alone*, even together.[8]

Alone, even while together. These words poignantly describe our contemporary plight. To be together, but not alone, begins with what Psalm 100 can teach us, that we belong to God, that we are not our own. The Psalter's songs of praise can help us acknowledge and address the loneliness, the lack of "social connectedness," the ruinous isolation that pervades our culture. They can help us acknowledge and address our rampant greed if we allow them to reach us and teach us another simple but radical lesson: namely, how to say "thank you," and not just to say it because it's good manners but because we are learning the countercultural lesson of gratitude.

Thankfulness and Grace

The title of Psalm 100 is "A Psalm of Thanksgiving" or "A Song for the Thank Offering," and two of its final three invitations to celebrate involve gratitude:

> Enter [God's] gates with thanksgiving . . .
> Give thanks to God.

Interestingly we may well hear the words "thank you" most often from cashiers at supermarkets or department stores. We get thanked most often for being good consumers, and this is not exactly a lesson in gratitude. Henri Nouwen said he had to go to Latin America to learn truly how to say "thank you."

> The word that I kept hearing, wherever I went was: *Gracias!* . . . *Gracias a Usted, a Dio muchos gracias*...thanks, thanks be to God, many thanks! . . .
>
> In many of the families I visited nothing was certain, nothing predictable, nothing totally safe. Maybe there would be food tomorrow, maybe there would be work tomorrow, maybe there would be peace tomorrow. Maybe, maybe not. . . . What I claim as a right, my friends in Bolivia and Peru received as a gift; . . . what for me goes by unnoticed became for them a new occasion to say thanks.
>
> And slowly I learned. I learned what I must have forgotten somewhere in my busy, well-planned, and very "useful" life. I learned that everything that is, is freely given by the God of love. All is grace. . . .
>
> A treasure lies hidden in the soul of Latin America, a spiritual treasure to be recognized as a gift for us who live in the illusion of power and self-control. It is the treasure of gratitude that can help us break through the walls of our individual and collective self-righteousness and can prevent us from destroying ourselves and our planet in the futile attempt to hold on to what we consider our own.[9]

The radical edge of Psalm 100 is not only that *we* are not our own but also that all of our stuff is not really our own either. The secret hidden in the lesson of gratitude is that it opens us up to living by grace. As Nouwen repeatedly said, "All is grace!"

How hard it is to live by grace in a world that instructs us to live by merit, to earn what we get, that good things come to those who *deserve* them. An advertisement selling pulpit robes to pastors bore the ironic caption: "You deserve the best!" Preachers face a dual challenge: to retool minds and hearts so they might grasp what grace and gratitude are all about, and simultaneously to fight tenaciously not to be infected by the very potent temptations to grasp for our just deserts for which we have labored so hard.

I Shall Not Want

How will our "I want" generation ever comprehend the first line of their own favorite Psalm, the Twenty-third? "The Lord is my shepherd, *I shall not want.*" Perhaps we should take that rendering quite literally.[10] Granted, the NRSV has preserved the KJV here and its archaic sense of the word "want." The line really means, "I shall lack nothing." Because the shepherd, God, provides food (green pastures), drink (still waters), and protection (right paths so as to avoid getting lost or killed), the Psalmist can say, "I shall lack nothing," just as "Restores my soul" means that the shepherd, God, keeps me alive.

The real issue for the Psalmist is *life.* Even in the midst of deep darkness that threatens with death, the Psalmist affirms that God gives life. The real issue for us too is life. What constitutes authentic life? Is it having the basic necessities (food, drink, shelter) as the Psalmist affirms? Or is it, as our culture teaches, getting, or at least trying to get, everything we want? When we pose the issue of Psalm 23 in this way, then we can legitimately argue that the Psalmist affirms something like this: "The LORD is my shepherd, and because God provides everything I *need* to live, I shall not *want* anything *more.*"

More. In advertising the subliminal and overt message is that *more* things bring life. In an ad for SkyTel, a very sophisticated paging or messaging system, we are reminded of a list of modern conveniences, like the microwave oven, the VCR, and the laptop computer. Now we say, "How did I live without it?" No such products even existed when we were children. But now we can't live without them? How did our grandparents survive? How did they manage such evidently full, content, and wise lives before the advent of gadgetry? Perhaps they knew the meaning of "I lack nothing. I shall not want."[11]

For Psalm 23, for the entire Bible, and for us, the issue is life. Is life something we can go out and get? Or is it something that must be given? If we go out and get life, we should be greedy. But if life does not consist in the abundance of possessions, as Jesus put it (Luke 12:15); if the ultimate security in life is something that can only be received as a gift, then our only option is to be grateful, and the address of our tutors is not on Madison Avenue but is sandwiched between Job and Proverbs in the Old Testament. "Give thanks to God" (Psalm 100:4). "The LORD is my shepherd, I shall not want" (Psalm 23:1). "Deliverance belongs to [that is, help comes from] the LORD" (Psalm 3:8).

Look at what else Psalms 100 and 23 have in common. Both cast God as the shepherd. In the ancient Near East and in the Bible, "shepherd" connotes power, not some idyllic sweetness. Kings were called the shepherds of their people. Not coincidentally, Psalm 100 follows a collection of Psalms (93-99, the so-called "enthronement Psalms") that explicitly announce that God reigns, that God rules the world.

Since Psalms 23 and 100 affirm God's sovereign power, we should notice that what they celebrate about God's power is how that sovereignty is manifested as goodness and faithful love. Psalm 100's last verse reads:

> For the LORD is good;
> [God's] steadfast love [*hesed*] endures forever,
> and [God's] faithfulness to all generations.
> (Psalm 100:5)

And the concluding verse of Psalm 23:

> Surely goodness and mercy
> [but better "steadfast love" = *hesed*]
> shall *pursue* [not "follow"] me
> all the days of my life,

and I shall dwell in the house of the LORD
my whole life long.

Here the Psalms of praise and assurance converge with the
Psalms of lament, both resonanting with the theme that God's
power is not sheer force, but is essentially love. *Ḥesed*, "steadfast
love" or "unfailing love," appears regularly in all types of Psalms.
In the laments, Psalmists appeal to God's *ḥesed*. In hymns of praise,
they celebrate God's *ḥesed*. In songs of assurance, they affirm their
trust in God's *ḥesed*.

Power as *Ḥesed*

Ḥesed is the key word of the Psalms and probably of the whole
Old Testament. Exodus 34:6 echoes throughout the canon:

The LORD, the LORD,
a God merciful and gracious,
slow to anger,
and abounding in steadfast love and faithfulness.

For the "I want" generation, power means force, and in particular
the ability—our ability—to get all those things we want. Given this
prevailing definition of power, it makes sense that we identify
codependency as a pervasive malady. There's something wrong
with us if we need other people or choose to depend upon them.
Now, there are real instances of destructive codependency. But in
her most disturbing insight about contemporary culture, Mary
Pipher points out that much of what we now identify as codependency should be reframed as *love*.[12]

It is not a total exaggeration to conclude that the Psalms finally
teach us that God is codependent. God has chosen to be in relationship with humankind and with the whole creation, even when
we humans choose to go our own way, even when our pursuit of
happiness is utterly self-centered rather than God-centered, when
we act in self-destructive ways instead of in life-receiving ways.
This is what *ḥesed* looks like. God is love. For us Christians, the
extent of God's loving involvement with us and with the world
culminates in the Incarnation. "The Word became flesh, . . . full of
grace and truth" (John 1:14 RSV), and the fourth Gospel here uses

125

the Greek equivalents of the Hebrew for "steadfast love and faithfulness" in Psalm 100:5.

More than a generation ago, Flannery O'Connor was increasingly disturbed by the growing secularism of American culture. Not surprisingly, a constant theme of her stories and novels is grace. In a letter to a friend, she wrote: "One of the awful things about writing when you are a Christian is that for you the ultimate reality is the Incarnation, the present reality is the Incarnation, and nobody believes in the Incarnation; that is, nobody in your audience."[13]

In a culture that teaches us that power is force and not love and that teaches us to pursue happiness autonomously, and in a time when it is becoming increasingly clear that the American dream of self-sufficiency is turning into a nightmare, the most crucial lesson the Psalms can teach us is to believe in the Incarnation.

Consider now a sermon on Psalm 47, a hymn of raucous celebration, that captures something of how the Incarnation redefines power as love. Such power is no less universal in its scope, but all the more tender for being so.

The Wreckage of Human Earthly Thrones: A Sermon on Psalm 47

Clap your hands? God has gone up with a shout? Trumpets? Sounds different from our worship.[14] Reminds me of the first time I preached at an African American church. The service was raucous, with clapping, shouting, singing, dancing. At first my jaw dropped. Then I re-collected my jaw and began to contemplate the tame words I had typed onto the piece of paper in my pocket—and I became nervous. Finally the preacher urged me into the pulpit, saying, "Brother Howell, come now, unfurl for us the scroll of heaven so that we might hear the angels sing." This made me very nervous.

But there is always an order to worship. In Israel, when it was time to clap, you clapped. When it was time to dance, you danced. There was time for silence. Even in Pentecostal-type churches today there is an order, a ritual—the way the hands are clapped, what the congregation says to the preacher, the mode and time of dancing. The key is always how we enter into the order of worship.

And the goal might be that we would be regarded like those early Methodists who were ridiculed for being "enthusiastic." It was considered bad form to get too enthusiastic. By the way, the word *enthusiastic* means "God has gotten into you." Our enthusiasm may not be dancing. It may be that most significant of acts in worship—what I call the "profound nod." Very enthusiastic!

Yet the item in Psalm 47 that intrigues me today is verse 8: "God reigns over the nations." Usually, when it comes to nations and the Lord, nations try to use the Lord, to co-opt and use God for their own purposes. It took Abraham Lincoln, not himself a church-goer, to recognize this in America. In his second inaugural, he said that both sides pray; both sides think God is on their side. But both sides are wrong. His climax: *The Almighty has his own purposes.*

The Lord is above all that nations do, and much of what they do is evil. We are troubled this week by India and Pakistan, testing nuclear weapons. At one time smaller powers couldn't compete, and we witnessed the rise of terrorism; now they have weapons of mass destruction. Governments just don't handle technology and power very well. As Einstein put it, technology can be "like an ax in the hands of a maniac." And yet we have to confess that India and Pakistan were tutored for decades by the United States and the Soviet Union, who played a dangerous game of one-upmanship, stockpiling nuclear warheads into six figures.

God is not pleased. God is not mocked. As an undergraduate I wrote a paper on Paul Tillich's view of idolatry. Tillich suggested that one idolatry is patriotism. No nation should claim our total allegiance—even our own. I love the United States. On the fifth grade trip to Washington, I reveled above all others in the words and monuments to Washington and Jefferson and Lincoln. But sin has infiltrated this country. The Clinton administration, despite doing much good, has made a mockery of good. But they learned well from their predecessors as well, even during the allegedly grand Reagan years, when Oliver North and John Poindexter and Ed Meese and others were indicted and lied.

That's just how it is with governments. But at the end of the day, "God reigns over the nations." God is not mocked; there is judgment. Karl Heim once wrote,

> The repeated collapse of every earthly imperialism is the most impressive demonstration of the fact that no divinization of any

127

earthly power can stand, that every absolutizing of any earthly absolute always carries within itself the seeds of death. God sets up his throne on the wreckage of human earthly thrones, and the history of the world is strewn with the wreckage of demolished imperialisms and smashed altars, whose debris reveals impressively the sole Lordship of God.[15]

Nations come and go. God gets the last word. Didn't you learn that great poem, "Ozymandias," when Shelley observed the toppled statue of Rameses II, the greatest of all Egyptian pharaohs?

> Two vast and trunkless legs of stone
> Stand in the desert. . . . Near them, on the sand,
> Half sunk, a shattered visage lies, whose frown,
> And wrinkled lip, and sneer of cold command,
> Tell that its sculptor well those passions read
> Which yet survive, stamped on these lifeless things, . . .
> Nothing beside remains. Round the decay
> Of that colossal wreck, boundless and bare
> The lone and level sands stretch far away.[16]

But there is another way to think about this: "God reigns over the nations." It is astonishing that in the age of satellites and instant telecommunication, when we should know more about the world than our predecessors, we are more woefully ignorant of geography and the peoples of the world than any previous generation. We do know about potential vacation destinations. But the world? and its people?

There was an earthquake this week—and I don't mean the little 3.2 tremor we had here. I mean the one in Afghanistan, the one where the paper dutifully reported that somewhere between 2,500 and 5,000 people were killed. The next morning I checked the paper for an update, a more exact death toll, stories of assistance. But *The Charlotte Observer* did not contain even once the word "Afghanistan" that day, nor the next, nor the next. All week I have talked with dozens of people—but I never heard anyone utter the word "Afghanistan." We did have an earthquake here—and it got my neighbors out into the street, full of hypotheses of what had happened: propane tank explosion? sonic boom? meteor? the rapture? I wish we were the kind of people who would pour out into the street to talk about thousands of our brothers and sisters in Afghanistan.

I can't prove this, but I don't think God even noticed our little 3.2 Richter scale tremor. But you can be sure that God, who reigns over the nations, noticed the horror in Afghanistan. And if you and I are remotely serious about serving the God who reigns over the nations, then we have to care. We have to weep. We have to share.

Jesus, after all, taught a new way of reigning. Pilate asked him, "Are you a king?" And he was—but he did not wield power by hoisting a bigger sword than the next guy and compelling others into submission. Rather, he invited people to a meal, to eat. And when they got there, he took up the trappings of his reign, a towel and basin, and washed their feet. After he said the blessing, he broke a piece of bread—and I believe that as he looked at it, it dawned on him what probably would happen to him the next day. For he knew that when you reign by washing feet and taking on the powers that be, they'll break you. I think when he gazed into the cup of wine, he saw blood. He hated bloodshed so much that he even shed his own blood. And reigned—by inviting all people everywhere, to a table, to eat, to taste a new way of living. And to me, that's something to clap about, to shout about, to sing about. *God reigns over the nations.*

Appendix

Music and Other Worship Resources

Within each liturgical tradition there will be appropriate avenues for worship planners to discover hymns and anthems that are appropriate to a given Psalm. Donald Spencer put together the *Hymn and Scripture Selection Guide* (with the lengthy subtitle: *A Cross-Reference of Scripture and Hymns with over 12,000 References for 380 Hymns and Gospel Songs* [Judson Press, Valley Forge, 1977]), and James Laster published two works with the Scarecrow Press, *Catalogue of Choral Music Arranged in Biblical Order* (1966) and *Catalogue of Vocal Solos and Duets Arranged in Biblical Order* (1984). Scarecrow has also published Jean Slater Edson's *Organ Preludes;* and Musicdata has a pair of great reference works by Thomas Nardone, *Organ Music in Print* and *Choral Music in Print.* Also see Arthur Wenk, *Musical Resources for the Revised Common Lectionary* (Scarecrow, 1994). A musician or minister can plunder these resources to find appropriate hymns, anthems, preludes.

On Psalmody, many resources exist out of various traditions, such as Maurice Frost, *English and Scottish Psalm and Hymn Tunes, c. 1543-1677* (Oxford, 1953); Frank Johnson Metcalf, *American Psalmody, or Titles of Books Containing Tunes Printed in America from 1721-1820* (New York: De Capo, 1968), a checklist of collections for choirs, children, congregations. James Litton, *The Plainsong Psalter* (Church Hymnal Corp., 1988) and Alec Wyton, *The Anglican Chant Psalter* (Church Hymnal Corp., 1987) are in the Anglican tradition. A supplementary resource to *The United Methodist Hymnal*'s Psalter is John Holbert, et al., *Psalms for Praise and Worship* (Abingdon Press, 1992), with a great index and creative materials for congregations. The Reformed tradition has *The Psalter: Psalms and Canticles for Singing* (Westminster/John Knox, 1993), with a diverse collection of everything from Gregorian to Hal Hopson to Taize style. The music of John-Michael Talbot, much of which is Psalm-oriented, is suitable not just for Roman Catholics but also for contemporary music fans. See Robin Leaver, et al., *Ways of Singing the Psalms* (Collins Liturgical Publications, 1984) and four works from Hopson: *10 Psalms* (Hope Publishing, 1986), *Ten More Psalms* (1990); *Eighteen Psalms for the Church Year* (1990); and *Psalm Refrains and Tones for the Common Lectionary*; as well as Jane Marshall, *Psalms Together: 6 Unison Antiphons for Choirs (or Cantor) and Congregation* (Choristers Guild, 1986). The hymnals, of course, frequently have Psalms for recitation and/or singing.

Psalter texts are plentiful, including *The Psalter: A New Version of Public Worship and Private Devotion* (Seabury, 1978) and Michael Morgan, *The Psalter for Christian Worship* (Witherspoon, 2000). Web sites treat many Psalms. For choral directors *www.choralnet.org* includes resources and many links, and the *musica* database is extremely valuable: *www.musicanet.org*.

Notes

1. An Invitation

1. Donald E. Gowan, *Reclaiming the Old Testament for the Christian Pulpit* (Atlanta: John Knox, 1980), p. 146.
2. David Buttrick, *Homiletic: Moves and Structures* (Philadelphia: Fortress, 1987), p. 478.
3. Robert Alter, *The Art of Biblical Poetry* (New York: Basic Books, 1985), p. 25.
4. From *Leaves of Grass*, quoted in Walter Brueggemann, *Finally Comes the Poet: Daring Speech for Proclamation* (Minneapolis: Fortress, 1989), p. viii.
5. Brueggemann, *Poet*, p. 3. Thomas Merton, in *Bread in the Wilderness* (New York: New Directions, 1953), pp. 53-54, argues that "the Psalms are poems, and poems have a meaning—although the poet has no obligation to make his meaning immediately clear to anyone who does not want to make an effort to discover it. . . . I believe . . . that the reason why so many fail to understand the Psalms . . . is that latent poetic faculties have never been awakened in their spirits by someone capable of pointing out to them that the Psalms really are poems."
6. Brueggemann, *Poet*, p. 17.
7. Merton, *Bread in the Wilderness*, p. 3.
8. C. H. Spurgeon saw this depth in a single Psalm. Looking at the lengthy Psalm 119, which "spread itself out before me like a vast, rolling prairie . . . seemed to me a great sea of holy teaching," he called "this sacred ode" a "little Bible, the Scriptures condensed . . . Holy Writ rewritten in holy emotions and actions" (*The Treasury of David* [Hendrickson, Mass.: Hendrickson, 1988], 3:131).
9. Karl Barth, *The Word of God and the Word of Man*, trans. Douglas Horton (New York: Harper & Bros., 1957), p. 36.
10. Ibid., p. 100.
11. Ibid., p. 108.
12. Ibid., p. 116.

2. A Great Tradition of Preaching

1. Karl Barth, *Call for God*, trans. A. T. Mackay (New York: Harper & Row, 1967), p. 40.
2. Ibid., pp. 43-44.
3. Ibid., pp. 44-45.
4. Dietrich Bonhoeffer, *Meditating on the Word*, ed. and trans. David Gracie (New York: Ballantine, 1986), pp. 49-54.
5. In 1940 he published *Psalms: The Prayerbook of the Bible*, trans. James H. Burtness (Minneapolis: Augsburg, 1970); see our discussion of this on p. 34.
6. Martin Niemöller, *God Is My Führer*, trans. Jane Lymburn (New York: Philosophical Library & Alliance Book Corp., 1941), pp. 100-101.

7. Ibid., p. 103.

8. Bonhoeffer, *Meditating on the Word*, pp. 81, 83.

9. Richard Lischer, *The Preacher King: Martin Luther King, Jr. and the Word That Moved America* (New York: Oxford University Press, 1995), p. 219.

10. Ibid., p. 224.

11. *Luther's Works: Lectures on the Psalms I*, vol. 10, trans. H. J. Bouman (St. Louis: Concordia, 1981), p. 23.

12. *Luther's Works*, vol. 14 (St. Louis: Concordia, 1958), pp. ix-x.

13. Ibid., pp. x, 45.

14. *Expositions on the Book of Psalms*, ed. Cleveland Coxe, *Nicene and Post-Nicene Fathers (NPNF)*, 1st series, vol. 8 (Grand Rapids: Eerdmans, 1974), p. 312.

15. *NPNF*, vol. 8, p. 632. Compare Augustine's *Confessions*, viii.5.10: "For in truth lust is made out of a perverse will, and when lust is served, it becomes habit, and when habit is not resisted, it becomes necessity. By such links, joined one to another, as it were—for this reason I have called it a chain—a harsh bondage held me fast."

16. *Homilies of St. Jerome*, trans. M. L. Ewald, vol. I, Fathers of the Church (Washington: Catholic University, 1964), p. 3.

17. Ibid., pp. 331-32.

18. Trevor A. Owen, *Lancelot Andrewes* (Boston: Twayne, 1981), p. 82.

19. *The Showing Forth of Christ: Sermons of John Donne*, ed. Edmund Fuller (New York: Harper & Row, 1964), p. 125.

20. Donne, *Showing Forth*, p. 228.

21. Christopher Hill, *The English Bible and the Seventeenth-Century Revolution* (New York: Penguin, 1994), p. 353.

22. Ibid., p. 54.

23. Ibid., p. 115.

24. Spurgeon, *Treasury of David*, 2:2:60.

25. Ibid., 2:2:233.

26. Ibid., 1:324.

27. Ibid.

28. Ibid., 1:329-30.

29. Ibid., 1:330.

30. Henry Ward Beecher, *Life Thoughts* (Boston: Phillips Sampson, 1858), pp. 8-10; in *The Psalms Through Three Thousand Years: Prayerbook of a Cloud of Witnesses* (Minneapolis: Fortress, 1993), pp. 362-65, William L. Holladay regards this as a pivotal moment in the history of Psalm 23 becoming "an American secular icon."

31. Phillips Brooks, *Addresses* (Chicago: W. B. Conkey, 1900), pp. 149-75, as quoted in *20 Centuries of Great Preaching*, ed. Clyde E. Fant and William M. Pinson (Waco: Word, 1971), 6:134-35.

32. Gardner C. Taylor, *Chariots Aflame* (Nashville: Broadman, 1988), p. 24.

33. Fleming Rutledge, *The Bible and the* New York Times (Grand Rapids: Eerdmans, 1998), pp. 151-56.

3. A View of Scripture

1. Diodore of Tarsus's prologue to the Psalter, translated by Brian E. Daley, S. J., Professor of Theology at the University of Notre Dame. Used by permission.

2. Thomas Merton, *Bread in the Wilderness* (New York: New Directions, 1953), p. 13.

3. Thomas Merton, *Praying the Psalms* (Collegeville: Liturgical Press, 1956), pp. 7-8.

4. Athanasius, "Letter to Marcellinus," ed. Clebsch, pp. 109, 111.

5. Calvin, *Commentary on the Book of Psalms*, vol. 1 (Edinburgh: Calvin Translation Society, 1845), p. xxxvii.

6. Diodore, translated by Daley.

7. Martin Luther, *Word and Sacrament I*, LW vol. 35, ed. E. Theodore Bachmann, trans. Charles M. Jacobs (Philadelphia: Fortress, 1960), pp. 255-56.

8. Calvin, *Commentary*, p. xxxvii.

9. Gerald T. Sheppard, "Theology and the Book of Psalms," *Interpretation* 46 (1992): 145.

10. Bonhoeffer, *Psalms: The Prayer Book of the Bible*, pp. 9-10. Burtness revised his translation for the *Dietrich Bonhoeffer Works* series (volume 5, published by Fortress in 1996), but the readability of the revision is inferior.

11. Bonhoeffer, *Psalms*, p. 11.

12. Ibid., pp. 14-15. Bonhoeffer joins a great chorus of preachers and teachers, from Origen to Augustine, to Luther and Spurgeon. We will need to wait until chapter 5 to say more about the "move" the preacher makes from the Psalms to the New Testament.

13. Walter Brueggemann, *Abiding Astonishment: Psalms, Modernity, and the Making of History* (Louisville: Westminster/John Knox Press, 1991), pp. 26, 28. He elaborates this theme, that the Psalms are not only responses to the reality of a relationship with God but also are expressions that help reshape that relationship, more fully in *Israel's Praise: Doxology Against Idolatry and Ideology* (Philadelphia: Fortress, 1988), pp. 3-28.

14. Erich Auerbach, *Mimesis: The Representation of Reality in Western Literature*, trans. Willard R. Trask (Princeton: Princeton University Press, 1953), p. 15.

15. Klaus Seybold, *Introducing the Psalms*, trans. R. G. Dunphy (Edinburgh: T. & T. Clark, 1990), p. 27; J. Clinton McCann, "The Psalms as Instruction," *Interpretation* 46 (1992): 117-28; McCann, *A Theological Introduction to the Book of Psalms: The Psalms as Torah* (Nashville: Abingdon Press, 1993); Brevard Childs, *Introduction to the Old Testament as Scripture* (Philadelphia: Fortress, 1979), p. 513; James Mays, "The Place of the Torah-Psalms in the Psalter," *JBL* 106/1 (1987): 3-12.

16. Calvin, *Commentary*, pp. xxxvii-xxxix.

17. See his autobiographical *Fear No Evil*, trans. Stefani Hoffman (New York: Random House, 1988), p. 229.

18. Bonhoeffer, *Psalms*, p. 25.

19. David Ford, *Self and Salvation: Being Transformed* (Cambridge: Cambridge University, 1999), p. 251.

20. Bonhoeffer, *Psalms*, pp. 10-11.

21. Richard Bauckham, *God Crucified: Monotheism & Christology in the New Testament* (Grand Rapids: Eerdmans, 1998), p. 72.

22. Ibid., p. 26.

23. See Jürgen Moltmann, *The Crucified God* (Minneapolis: Fortress, 1993), pp.

145-53, 220-78, and a sober evaluation by William Stacy Johnson, *The Mystery of God: Karl Barth and the Postmodern Foundations of Theology* (Louisville: Westminster John Knox, 1997), pp. 106-10.

24. Calvin, *Commentary*, pp. xl-xli. For a full analysis of what this means for the educational life of the church, see Richard Robert Osmer, *A Teachable Spirit: Recovering the Teaching Office in the Church* (Louisville: Westminster John Knox, 1990).

25. Merton, *Bread in the Wilderness*, p. 75. Earlier he had written, "The Holy Ghost prays in the Liturgy and when we pray with the Liturgy the Holy Ghost, the Spirit of Christ, prays in us. He teaches us how to pray by praying in us. He not only gives us words to say and sing, He also sings them in our hearts" (p. 41).

26. Preached by James Howell at Davidson United Methodist Church, August 1998. On this Sunday, the bulletin included an introduction to the Psalm:

> *A National Lament.* Psalm 85 is one of the prayers in the Bible that originally functioned as a national prayer for God's mercy and help. In times of national crisis, a great fast would be proclaimed. Citizens would gather in cities, and pray in unison for change. They would repent, plead for forgiveness, ask for a restoration of the ways of God, and search for divine intervention. You might read Psalm 44, Psalm 74, Isaiah 58, and Jeremiah 36 for other public prayers.

Jane Marshall's moving "Psalm of Peace" proved to be the perfect choral anthem, and "Let There Be Peace on Earth" served as a helpful closing hymn.

27. Mark Helprin, *Winter's Tale* (New York: Pocket Books, 1983), p. 253.

28. William Shakespeare, *Romeo and Juliet*, act II, scene 2.

4. The Exploration of Imagery

1. Spurgeon, *Treasury of David*, 2:2:302.

2. Spurgeon, *Treasury of David*, 1:58-59.

3. Gerald Kennedy, "The Man Who Walked Through Time," in *20 Centuries of Great Preaching*, ed. Clyde Fant & Wm. Pinson, vol. 12 (Waco: Word, 1971), pp. 155-58.

4. Spurgeon, *Treasury of David*, 1:237. In the Middle Ages, Perez of Valencia († 1480) tied Psalm 90's image of God as a refuge to John 19:34, and considers the wounds in Christ's hands, feet, and side as the special clefts in the rock, or hiding places for Christians.

5. Spurgeon, *Treasury of David*, 2:2:61.

6. Tom Beaudoin, *Virtual Faith: The Irreverent Spiritual Quest of Generation X* (San Francisco: Jossey-Bass, 1998), p. 47.

7. Augustine, *On Christian Doctrine*, II.6, trans. D. W. Robertson (Indianapolis: Bobbs-Merrill, 1958), p. 37.

8. Garrett Greene, *Imagining God: Theology and the Religious Imagination* (San Francisco: Harper & Row, 1989), p. 83.

9. T. S. Eliot, "The Use of Poetry and the Use of Criticism" (1933), in *Selected Prose of T. S. Eliot*, ed. Frank Kermode (New York: Harcourt Brace Jovanovich, 1975), p. 93.

10. We know a good bit about the patterns and rhythms common in Hebrew

poetry—but strophic conventions figure more prominently in the commentaries than in any sermon. A very clever preacher might pick up on the 3 + 2 rhythm of a Psalm like 27, that elegaic pattern used in many laments, whereby we hear a longer three-beat line, then a shorter pair of beats, almost like a sigh. Many Psalms use alliteration and other phonic devices, which are reproduced into English only with terrible complications. But the preacher might learn from the Psalmist how to use language deliberately, dramatically. Spurgeon is the stellar example. Even when we are not preaching on poetic texts, there is wisdom to writing a sermon, not in linear fashion as we would write prose, but in actual lines with rhythm and pattern, appearing more like poetry on the page, reflective of the way we actually talk. See G. Robert Jacks, *Just Say the Word! Writing for the Ear* (Grand Rapids: Wm. B. Eerdmans, 1996).

11. *Homilies of St. Jerome*, vol. 1, trans. M. L. Ewald, Fathers of the Church 48 (Washington: Catholic University of America, 1964), pp. 359-60. Jerome is following Augustine in this line of thought.

12. Spurgeon, *Treasury of David*, 3:2:116.

13. T. S. Eliot wrote that "the poem's existence is somewhere between the writer and the reader; it has a reality which is not simply the reality of what the writer is trying to 'express,' or of his experience of writing it. . . . What a poem means is as much what it means to others as what it means to the author." He notes how Shakespeare repeatedly in using a word "will give a new meaning or extract a latent one; again and again the right imagery saturated while it lay in the depths of Shakespeare's memory, will rise like Anadyomene from the sea." *Selected Prose*, pp. 80, 88, 90.

14. James L. Mays, *Psalms*, Interpretation: A Bible Commentary for Teaching and Preaching (Louisville: John Knox, 1994), pp. 23-24.

15. Walter Brueggemann, *The Message of the Psalms: A Theological Commentary* (Minneapolis: Augsburg, 1984), p. 53.

16. Susan Howatch, *Absolute Truths* (New York: Fawcett Crest, 1994), p. 473. Paul Ricoeur has noted how the Psalms demonstrate the fragility and vulnerability of life in *Oneself as Another* (Chicago: Univ. of Chicago, 1992), p. 22; see also Ford, *Self and Salvation*, pp. 125-29.

17. Leslie F. Brandt, *Psalms Now*, rev. ed. (St. Louis: Concordia, 1996), n.p.

18. *Halford Luccock Treasury*, ed. Robert E. Luccock (New York: Abingdon Press, 1963), p. 58. Luccock taught preaching at Yale from 1928 to 1953.

19. Ernesto Cardenal, "I Cry in the Night from the Torture Chamber," from "Risk" 1973 (IX/3), WCC Publications, World Council of Churches, Geneva, Switzerland, and *Mission Trends No. 3: Third World Theologies*, ed. Gerald H. Anderson and Thomas F. Stransky (New York: Paulist, 1976), p. 39.

20. Walter Brueggemann, *The Psalms and the Life of Faith*, ed. Patrick D. Miller (Minneapolis: Fortress Press, 1995), p. 34.

21. Nicholas Lash, "Human Experience and the Knowledge of God," in *Theology on the Way to Emmaus* (London: SCM, 1986), p. 143.

22. Robert McCracken, "Beware of Melancholy," in *20 Centuries of Great Preaching*, 12:65-69.

23. Martin Niemöller, *Dachau Sermons*, trans. Robert H. Pfeiffer (New York: Harper & Row, 1946), p. 6.

24. McCracken, "Beware," pp. 65-69.

25. Richard Schickel, *The World of Goya, 1746-1828* (New York: Time-Life, 1968), p. 109; quoted in Simon Blackburn, *Think: A Compelling Introduction to Philosophy* (Oxford: Oxford Univ., 1999), p. 13. In *The Complete Etchings of Goya* (New York: Crown, 1943), p. 19, it is translated, "Imagination deserted by reason creates impossible, useless thoughts. United with reason, Imagination is the mother of all art and the source of all its beauty."

26. Augustine, *On Christian Doctrine*, II.32, p. 68.

27. Reinhold Niebuhr, "Humour and Faith," in *Discerning the Signs of the Times* (New York: Charles Scribner's Sons, 1946), pp. 111-31.

28. Facility in Hebrew can be of help in preaching the Psalms; without it, commentaries may still alert the preacher to peculiarities in the original. We are reminded of Merton, who said, "I imagine that every contemplative would, at some time or other, wish that he could chant the Psalms in the same language in which they were chanted by Jesus on this earth, and in which He quoted them when He was dying on the Cross!" (*Bread in the Wilderness*, p. 54).

29. Great photos and old lithographs appear in David Roberts, *The Holy Land: Yesterday and Today* (New York: Stewart, Tabori & Chang, 1994). A particularly helpful guide book is Jerome Murphy O'Connor, *The Holy Land: an Oxford Archaeological Guide from the Earliest Times to 1700*, 4th ed. (New York: Oxford Univ., 1998). A scholarly book that studies iconography in the Middle East from biblical times is Othmar Keel, *The Symbolism of the Biblical World: Ancient Near Eastern Iconography and the Book of Psalms* (New York: Crossroad, 1978).

30. Spurgeon, *Treasury of David*, 3:71.

31. Mother Teresa, *A Simple Path* (New York: Ballantine, 1995), pp. 99-100.

32. Paul Ricoeur, "Toward a Hemeneutic of the Idea of Revelation," in *Essays on Biblical Interpretation*, ed. Lewis S. Mudge (Philadelphia: Fortress, 1980), p. 101.

33. Daniel Hardy and David Ford, *Praising and Knowing God* (Philadelphia: Westminster, 1985), p. 1.

34. Ibid., p. 14.

35. Brueggemann takes notice of the storyteller in Leon Uris's novel, *Trinity*, who says, "Aye, Seamus, there was no Brotherhood, no ability to rage, I became so broken with frustration I did what I swore would never happen. I was driven out of Ireland. Ah, not by the British but by the apathy of our own people" *Life of Faith*, p. 159, n. 28).

36. Preached by Howell in May 1997 at Davidson. Spurgeon, commenting on the thirst expressed in the first verse, wrote, "It is a sweet bitterness. The next best thing to living in the light of the Lord's love is to be unhappy till we have it. . . . When it is as natural for us to long for God as for an animal to thirst, it is well with our souls, however painful our feelings" (*Treasury of David*,1:2:271). This Psalm was also a childhood favorite of Bonhoeffer; we have a sermon he preached at Finkenwalde in 1935 on this text (*Meditating on the Word*, pp. 55-61).

37. Pat Conroy, *The Lords of Discipline* (New York: Bantam, 1982), p. 55.

38. Augustine, *Confessions* 1. 1.i.

39. Quoted by Henri Nouwen, *The Road to Daybreak: A Spiritual Journey* (New York: Doubleday, 1988), p. 117.

40. *The Dialogue,* Classics of Western Spirituality (Mahwah, N.J.: Paulist Press, 1980), p. 365.

41. Joseph Cardinal Bernardin, *The Gift of Peace: Personal Reflections* (Chicago: Loyola, 1997), p. 67.

42. Henry David Thoreau, *Walden* (New York: Bantam Books, 1962), p. 172.

43. Amos Wilder, "Electric Chimes or Rams' Horns," in *Grace Confounding* (Philadelphia: Fortress, 1972), p. 13.

44. T. S. Eliot, "Choruses from 'The Rock'" vi, in *T. S. Eliot: Collected Poems, 1909–1962* (New York: Harcourt Brace Javanovich, 1963), p. 160.

5. The Dynamics of Movement

1. Particularly helpful are Patrick D. Miller, *They Cried to the Lord: The Form and Theology of Biblical Prayer* (Minneapolis: Fortress, 1994), and the fascinating studies of John Eaton, *The Psalms Come Alive: Capturing the Voice & Art of Israel's Songs* (Downers Grove: InterVarsity, 1984), and Mark S. Smith, Psalms: *The Divine Journey* (Mahwah: Paulist, 1987), both of which paint vivid portraits of Israel's vibrant life of worship.

2. A wonderful book illustrating the feel and archaeological remains of ancient Jerusalem is Hershel Shanks, *Jerusalem: An Archaeological Biography* (New York: Random House, 1995).

3. Five of them are included in the series *20 Centuries of Great Preaching*, vol. 11.

4. Spurgeon, *Treasury of David* 1:1-2. Augustine attends to a similar sequence in his *Confessions,* viii 5.10: "Lust is made out of a perverse will, and when lust is served, it becomes a habit, and when habit is not resisted, it becomes necessity," trans. John K. Ryan (Garden City, N. J.: Image Books, 1960), p. 188.

5. Ibid., 1:56.

6. Walter Brueggemann, "The Formfulness of Grief," *Interpretation* 31 (1977): 263-75, compared the structure of the lament to Elizabeth Kübler-Ross's discernment of the stages of grieving and dying (denial, anger, bargaining, depression, acceptance); pastors and counselors understand well that our ability to name and thereby get some handle on the dark vortex of agony is itself salvific.

7. Wade Clark Roof, *A Generation of Seekers: The Spiritual Journeys of the Baby Boom Generation* (New York: HarperCollins, 1993), p. 67.

8. Douglas John Hall, *Professing the Faith: Christian Theology in a North American Context* (Minneapolis: Fortress, 1993), pp. 253-300.

9. Spurgeon, *Treasury of David*, 1:153.

10. Ibid., 1:59.

11. Brueggemann, *Life of Faith,* pp. 9-15.

12. See the powerful sermon by Barbara Brown Taylor, "The Gift of Disillusionment," in *God in Pain: Teaching Sermons on Suffering* (Nashville: Abingdon Press, 1998), pp. 17-21.

13. Hardy and Ford, *Praising and Knowing God,* p. 97.

14. Christopher Lasch, *The True and Only Heaven: Progress and Its Critics* (New York: W. W. Norton, 1991), p. 81.

15. Brueggemann, *Message of the Psalms,* p. 67.

16. See James C. Howell, *Servants, Misfits and Martyrs: Saints and Their Stories* (Nashville: Upper Room, 2000), especially chapter 5 on the historic task of preaching.

17. *Self and Salvation*, p. 121.

18. Ibid., p. 127. He goes on to note that "it is a feature of good liturgical texts that they allow large numbers of diverse people to identify themselves through them. . . . The liturgical 'I' suggests a conception of selfhood . . . which does not simply see itself as separate from all the other selves and groups worshipping through the same liturgy or the Psalms. Seeing oneself as one among the many who indwell the Psalms by singing them encourages one to consider how the others might be related to oneself."

19. Diodore, translated by Daley.

20. Spurgeon, *Treasury of David*, 1:353.

21. Gerald Wilson, "The Shape of the Book of Psalms," *Interpretation* 46 (1992): 129-42.

22. Brueggemann, *Life of Faith*, p. 197.

23. Preached by Howell, July 1997, on the text Spurgeon called "the narrative of a great soul-battle, a spiritual Marathon" (*Treasury of David*, 2:247). When we selected a date to preach on Psalm 73, we could not have imagined how timely it would prove to be, with several painful losses in the congregation occurring just days before. With a raw edge of grief and minds full of questions, we gathered for worship, with a prayer of confession that was built upon the first portion of the text: "O God, you are our strength, even when our faith fails. We wear our pride like a necklace. We clothe ourselves in judgment without mercy. We covet that which will not lead us closer to you. We turn our backs to your gaze. Forgive us. Work within us, until there is nothing on earth that we desire more than you." The bulletin insert provided some background information:

> Psalm 73 is one of the most eloquent, and moving, of all the Psalms. It was Martin Buber's favorite; he asked that verses 23 and 24 be inscribed on his tombstone. The last of Charles Wesley's 6500 hymns was written on his deathbed, and it was inspired by Psalm 73. It begins with a little motto, one of those familiar religious sayings everyone knows and loves: "Surely God is good to the pure in heart." But this Psalmist has a few questions, and they are intensely personal. Verses 1-12 are an outburst, a cry against the unfairness of life. The Psalmist, in some ways like Job, has been faithful to God—but has enjoyed no great "good" from God. Instead he has faced constant sickness and poverty—all made worse by the fact that he has to look upon wicked people who are all healthy and prosperous. Aren't there rewards for goodness and punishments for wickedness? Why does it seem reversed so often? Verses 13-17 form a turning point, as the Psalmist manages not to jettison his faith in God. Somehow, going to the sanctuary of God changes everything. Verses 18-28 then form one of the most beautiful expressions of faith in God, love for God, intimacy with God, in all the Bible.

We sang the Cleland McAfee hymn, "Near to the Heart of God," and the choir did Joseph Swain's beautiful anthem, "O Thou, in Whose Presence." Instead of a responsive reading, we recruited our best lectors who recited the entire Psalm reflectively. Then came the sermon, aided by liberal borrowings from McCann's *New Interpreter's Bible* commentary, vol. 4 (Nashville: Abingdon Press, 1996).

24. G. K. Chesterton, "The Eternal Revolution," *Orthodoxy* (1908).

25. Peter Collier, *The Roosevelts: An American Saga* (New York: Simon & Schuster, 1994), p. 63.

26. Charles Wesley, 1788.

27. Rian Malan, *My Traitor's Heart: A South African Exile Returns to Face His Country, His Tribe, and His Conscience* (New York: Vintage, 1990), p. 409.

6. The Pursuit of Happiness

1. Chapters 6, 7, and 8 are adapted from the Todd Lectures given at Memphis Theological Seminary in 1998 by McCann.

2. Hans-Joachim Kraus, *Theology of the Psalms*, trans. Keith Crim (Minneapolis: Augsburg, 1986). More accessible for the preacher might be Brueggemann, *Message of the Psalms* or McCann, *A Theological Introduction*.

3. Quoted in Eugene Kennedy, "A Dissenting Voice: Catholic Theologian David Tracy," *New York Times Magazine*, November 9, 1986, p. 25.

4. Walker Percy, *Lost in the Cosmos: The Last Self-Help Book* (New York: Washington Square, 1983), p. 178.

5. Mary Pipher, *The Shelter of Each Other: Rebuilding Our Families* (New York: G. P. Putnam's Sons, 1996), p. 26.

6. James L. Mays, *Psalms*, Interpretation: A Bible Commentary for Teaching and Preaching (Louisville: John Knox, 1994) p. 40.

7. William Willimon, "Sixth Sunday After Epiphany," *Homiletics*, February 15, 1998, p. 27.

8. Mays, *Psalms*, pp. 43-44.

9. Gary Chamberlain, *The Psalms: A New Translation for Prayer and Worship* (Nashville: Upper Room, 1984), p. 26.

10. *St. Louis Post-Dispatch*, October 7, 1993.

11. Pipher, *Shelter of Each Other*, p. 26, emphasis added.

12. Robert Putnam, *The Journal of Democracy* 6/1 (January 1995): 65-78. See also his more recent and expansive analysis, *Bowling Alone: The Collapse and Revival of American Democracy* (New York: Simon & Schuster, 2000).

13. M. Douglas Meeks, *God the Economist: The Doctrine of God and Political Economy* (Minneapolis: Fortress, 1989), pp. 47-73.

14. Reinhold Niebuhr, *The Nature and Destiny of Man*, vol. 1 (New York: Charles Scribner's Sons, 1941), p. 191.

15. Reinhold Niebuhr, *The Irony of American History* (New York: Charles Scribner's Sons, 1952).

16. Pipher, *Shelter of Each Other*, p. 81.

17. Anne Lamott, *Bird by Bird: Some Instructions on Writing and Life* (New York: Anchor Books, 1994), p. 108.

18. Ibid., pp. 180-81.

19. John Dominic Crossan, *Jesus: A Revolutionary Biography* (San Francisco: Harper San Francisco, 1994), p. 54.

20. Preached by Howell on May 10, 1997, at Davidson. That day the choir sang Franz Joseph Haydn's "The Heavens Are Telling," from *The Creation*. The congregation sang "This Is My Father's World," and we concluded the service with the

Philip Bliss oldie, "Wonderful Words of Life." The printed prayer of confession picked up on the text, reading: "O God of glory, your law is perfect; it revives our souls. Your precepts are right; they rejoice our hearts. Forgive us for straying from your desire for us. Forgive us for the sins that we knowingly commit. And forgive us for the sins that remain hidden from us. Free us from our bondage to our sins, so that we, with the heavens, might tell the glory of God."

A bulletin insert read:

C. S. Lewis called Psalm 19 "the greatest poem in the Psalter and one of the greatest lyrics in the world." Its threefold structure sets an example for our own spirituality: (a) Verses 1-6 extol the grandeur of nature. (b) Verses 7-11 praise the greatness of God's law. (c) Verses 12-15 are a deeply personal prayer. The interconnections are profound. God, who ordered the world, also in his mercy gives us directives for how to live in it and take care of it. Just as we are awed by the beauty of nature, we may pause to explore the beauty of God's law. And nature and law are never just out there, somehow removed from us, something we just observe. Rather, they compel us to pray, to get involved, to offer ourselves, to become sharers in what God is about in the world.

Torah. The Hebrew word translated as "law" is *Torah*—and *Torah* does not mean "law" in the way we construe "law." *Torah* means "way" or "path," with the connotation that we are on a journey, going somewhere, armed with directions, instructions. God saved the Israelites from Egypt, and led them, not off to a luxuriant island for a vacation, but promptly to Mt. Sinai to learn God's laws. Moses received them, and brought them to the people, as a pattern for how to live as God's saved people—or, as Nahum Sarna put it, "how to stay free." Psalm 19 praises the Torah as perfect, sure, right, pure, clean, true, more valuable than gold, tastier than honey, capable of giving life, the source of wisdom. Three translation improvements: verse 7 should say, "The way of the Lord is all-encompassing, restoring human life." And verse 11, which sounds a bit threatening, can be read "By them is your servant instructed; there is great consequence (instead of 'reward') in keeping them." And therefore, verse 13 concludes like this: "Then I will be whole (not 'blameless'), and acquitted (instead of 'innocent') of great transgression."

Jesus, Paul, and the Law. Many Christians mistakenly think that law and grace are somehow antithetical, and that because of Christ there is no law, no requirements, but sheer and total mercy from God, no matter what we may do. It is true that Jesus died, and that salvation is something we are utterly incapable of earning. But the sense of the New Testament is clearly that because of the great gift of mercy in Christ, we are if anything more motivated and eager to adhere to the ways of God; we are finally enabled, empowered, set free to do God's will. Jesus said, "I came not to abolish the law and prophets but to fulfill them" (Matthew 5:17). We live "by every word that comes from the mouth of God" (Matthew 4:4). Paul said, "We uphold the law" (Romans 3:31). The letter to the Romans, so full of grace, builds up to chapters 12 and following that tell us much about the demands and shape of the Christian life. The problem is "legalism"—where we begin to use the law as a fence to exclude or judge others, as a weapon of manipulation, or as a prop for our egos (also known as "self-righteousness"). The antidote to an immoral society is precisely the same as the antidote to a smug, holier-than-thou goodness: to look to God's word as a precious, merciful gift, to be treasured and savored.

7. The Problem of Pain

1. Lamott, *Bird by Bird*, p. 89.

2. Quoted in his comments on Psalm 3 by Eugene A. Peterson, *Answering God: The Psalms as Tools for Prayer* (San Francisco: Harper & Row, 1989), p. 36.

3. James L. Mays, "Psalm 13," *Interpretation* 34 (1980): 282.

4. Robert Frost (in "A Masque of Reason") imagined God expressing gratitude

to Job for setting God and all of us free from bondage to the doctrine of retribution.

5. Wendy Farley, *Tragic Vision and Divine Compassion: A Contemporary Theodicy* (Louisville: Westminster/John Knox, 1990), pp. 118-19.

6. When we ask, "Why do bad things happen to good people?" we usually rank ourselves as good. Interestingly, from a historical perspective, it has been only in the era when we think we have done so well that we have begun to question God for being inept; see Gerhard O. Forde, *On Being a Theologian of the Cross: Reflections on Luther's Heidelberg Disputation, 1518* (Grand Rapids: Eerdmans, 1997), pp. 84-85, no. 14. He quotes Hannah Arendt, who said, "When men could no longer *praise*, they turned their greatest conceptual efforts to *justifying* God and His Creation in theodicies" (Arendt, *The Life of the Mind*, [New York: Harcourt Brace Jovanovich, 1977], 2:97).

7. The very last line of Dante's *Divine Comedy* speaks of "the Love that moves the sun and the other stars" (*The Portable Dante*, trans. Mark Musa [New York: Penguin, 1995], p. 585).

8. Pipher, *Shelter of Each Other*, p. 93.

9. Ibid., p. 32, emphasis added. Compare the insightful analysis of Christopher Lasch, who noted how consumerism "promotes an ethic of hedonism," how advertising "tries to create new demands and new discontents that can be assuaged only by the consumption of commodities," how "advertising and the logic of consumerism . . . govern the depiction of reality in the mass media," how shopping "seems to present itself as a form of therapy," and "serves as a means of alleviating loneliness, dispelling boredom, and relieving depression. They don't really need what they are shopping for. Often they don't even know what they're after" (in *True and Only Heaven*, pp. 518-22).

10. Walker Percy, *The Last Gentleman* (New York: Ivy Books, 1966), pp. 73-74.

11. Pipher, *The Shelter of Each Other*, p. 143.

12. Brueggemann, "The Costly Loss of Lament," in *Life of Faith*, pp. 98-111.

13. H. H. Schmid, "Creation, Righteousness, and Salvation: 'Creation Theology' as the Broad Horizon of Biblical Theology," in *Creation in the Old Testament*, ed. Bernhard W. Anderson, Issues in Theology and Religion 6 (Philadelphia: Fortress, 1984), p. 114.

14. See Elsa Tamez, *The Amnesty of Grace: Justification by Faith from a Latin American Perspective*, trans. Sharon H. Ringe (Nashville: Abingdon Press, 1993), pp. 134-140.

15. Preached by McCann at First Presbyterian Church, Gastonia, North Carolina, October 12, 1997.

16. Howard Owen, *Littlejohn* (New York: Villard Books, 1993), pp. 118-19.

8. The Cause for Celebration

1. Reinhold Niebuhr, *Leaves from the Notebook of a Tamed Cynic* (San Francisco: Harper & Row, 1929/1980), pp. 147-48, emphasis added.

2. See especially Brueggemann, *Israel's Praise: Doxology Against Idolatry and Ideology* (Philadelphia: Fortress, 1988).

3. Brueggemann, "Psalm 146: Psalm for the Nineteenth Sunday after

Pentecost," *No Other Foundation* 8/1 (summer 1987): 28. See a full discussion in his *Theology of the Old Testament: Testimony, Dispute, Advocacy* (Minneapolis: Fortress, 1997), pp. 450-91.

4. The most famous example being the tetragrammaton, *YHWH*, which perpetually was "read" as *Adonai*, "Lord," given the unspeakable sanctity of the divine name. For many interesting examples, see G. E. Weil, "Qere-kethibh," *The Interpreter's Dictionary of the Bible*, supplementary volume (Nashville: Abingdon Press, 1976), pp. 716-23.

5. The phrase is Mary Pipher's, in *Shelter of Each Other*, p. 180.

6. Brian Wren, "We Are Not Our Own." Copyright 1985, Hope Publishing Company, Carol Stream, Illinois.

7. M. Scott Peck, *People of the Lie: The Hope for Healing Human Evil* (New York: Simon & Schuster, 1983), pp. 167-68, emphasis added.

8. J. California Cooper, "Friends, Anyone?" in *The Matter Is Life* (New York: Anchor Books, 1991), p. 68.

9. Henri Nouwen, *¡Gracias!: A Latin American Journal* (San Francisco: Harper & Row, 1983), pp. 187-88. Nouwen had this lesson deepened when he began working with Jean Vanier's L'Arche communities that serve adults with severe disabilities; see *The Road to Daybreak: A Spiritual Journey* (New York: Image, 1990).

10. See McCann, *Theological Introduction*, pp. 128-29.

11. Allan Bloom (in *The Closing of the American Mind* [New York: Simon & Schuster, 1987], p. 60) wrote,

My grandparents were ignorant people by our standards, and my grandfather held only lowly jobs. But their home was spiritually rich because all the things done in it... found their origin in the Bible's commandments, and their explanation in the Bible's stories and the commentaries on them, and had their imaginative counterparts in the deeds of the myriad of exemplary heroes. . . . My grandparents found reasons for the existence of their family and the fulfillment of their duties in serious writings, and they interpreted their special sufferings with respect to a great and ennobling past. . . . I do not believe that my generation, my cousins who have been educated in the American way, all of whom are M.D.s or Ph.D.s, have any comparable learning. When they talk about heaven and earth, the relations between men and women, parents and children, the human condition, I hear nothing but cliches, superficialities, the material of satire.

12. Pipher, *Shelter of Each Other*, pp. 137-38.

13. Flannery O'Connor, *The Habit of Being: Letters of Flannery O'Connor*, ed. Sally Fitzgerald (New York: Farrar, Straus, Giroux, 1979), p. 92.

14. Preached by Howell, July 1997. The congregation sang Charles Wesley's "Praise the Lord who Reigns Above," and the choir performed the splendid John Rutter setting of Psalm 47, "O Clap Your Hands."

15. Karl Heim, *The Transformation of the Scientific World View* (New York: Harper & Brothers, 1953), p. 21.

16. Percy Bysshe Shelley, "Ozymandias."